Captain's Stories:
Tales of Travel

Discovering the past – experiencing the future

Captain Paul Eschenfelder

@ 2015, Paul Eschenfelder

www.captaincruising.net

Except as provided in applicable law, no part of this publication may be reproduced, stored in a retrieval system or transmitted in any form or by any means without the prior written permission of the author.

Although every precaution has been taken to verify the accuracy of the information contained herein, the author assumes no responsibility for any errors or omissions. No liability is assumed for damages that may result from the use of information contained within.

Eschenfelder, Paul , 1949 -

Captain's Stories: Tales of Travel

ISBN: 9781503259683

Library of Congress Control Number: 2014921508

CreateSpace Independent Publishing Platform, North Charleston, SC

1. Travel 2. History

For Ann Marie, the First Mate

Table of Contents

The Pacific

Swell, page 8

The Spy, page 16

Death of Cook, page 22

Rainbow Warrior, page 29

Battery Randolph, page 36

The Mediterranean

Pharaoh's Dream, page 43

Father, page 53

Marathon Man, page 58

St. Mark's Bones, page 67

One Onion, page 78

The Atlantic

Vikings in North America, page 90

Mutiny on the Baltic, page 99

Young Winston, page 110

Fear of Bojador, page 123

Volcano in the Back Yard, page 135

Preface

Perhaps they can't go. Or, perhaps they just haven't been. Yet. It was Mark Twain who popularized the idea that "...travel broadens a man". And entertains. And educates a person.

Why do cruise ship passengers, aboard for several days at sea, crowd the rail to see landfall?

Why do airplane passengers, after years of flying experience, still peer out the windows as their aircraft ascends and descends?

Why do we demand of astronauts an explanation of "...what's it like..." to be in space?

Is the experience of "new", or unexplored, at least by us, the compelling question?

And when we finally see "it", whatever "it" is, do we know it? Or as we gaze at "it", do we still wonder what "it" is all about?

Years at sea and in the air still have me peering out the window, turning the corner to see what is there and asking the question "...what's it all about?" I find I'm not the only one. People from all over the globe come to hear what "it" is all about - to explore more with their minds as they explore with their bodies. Their search is to reach that "ah-ha" moment when, suddenly, "it" all comes together: what they see couples with what they know. And, at that moment, they meet Mark Twain.

Read about some of those many places worldwide which so interest travelers. It is just a glimpse of people who made history, or the places where our world changed.

But, for some readers, it may provide just enough "ah-ha" to keep them moving forward, turning corners.

Paul Eschenfelder

At Sea

September, 2014

The Pacific

Swell

It does seem a cruel joke. Mother Nature must need a real belly laugh from time to time. The sweater over an aloha shirt, the undershirt under an aloha shirt – it's just not right. A cruise from San Diego to Hawaii is a dream of sunshine and tropical breezes. Yet that is not where the MS *Statendam* finds itself. The haberdashery of its passengers must conform.

Scotsmen on board feel the chill and damp of home. They search the sky, pleading for the hidden sun. The Dutch wander the decks with dour faces, complaining of wasted money. By mid-April winter should be over, the sun shining, the sun tan oil flowing like a river. But not so. None had realized the trap into which they had fallen.

The North Pacific Current starts in the Bay of Alaska, a name which in itself should serve as a warning. It flows south on its never ending journey to Mexico, brushing the California coast with the balm of the Mediterranean. The onshore breezes cool California and inspire chambers of commerce all along the coast. But the *Statendam* must cross this current and that which is pleasant while ashore is downright cold while at sea. Strong high pressure in the central Pacific births the sea breeze – the trade winds, the trades. The trades fan the cool current. The current builds into a swell. The swells grow to 10-12 feet and strike the *Statendam* on the beam, giving us a chilly, rocky ride. The elevator lobbies grow containers of doggy bags, discretely hung by the crew. These doggy bags are not for your take home snacks.

Still, it is a 55,000 ton cruise ship equipped with modern stabilizers and a fully stocked compliment of bars. So what if the ship's shops are sold out of Dramamine and sweat shirts. Hey, we are on our way to Hawaii. Just like the ancient voyagers. Almost.

The long Pacific swell meant something else one thousand years ago. Then, to the Stone Age navigators of the voyaging canoes, it meant their only compass, their only means of determining direction. Over thousands of miles the swells had formed. They would not be dissuaded from their course by mere storms, capricious light winds or mighty hurricanes. These Polynesian canoe navigators, or wayfinders, bet their lives that the swells would stay true in their direction. At night the stars were the friends of the wayfinder, but by day it was the swell. With no compass to guide him during the day, the wayfinder needed a manner in which to maintain his course. If he studied the swell, as his father, his grandfather and his grandfather before him had taught him, he could ensure the bow of his canoe, all day long, maintained the same relative position to the swell. The swell would never change. If the wayfinder noticed that the swell had moved forward toward the bow or aft on the beam, he knew his canoe had turned and that he must correct his course. Then by night, the stars would rise to confirm his course and congratulate the wayfinder on his fidelity to his course and craft.

Wayfinding, or open ocean navigating, led people of the western Pacific into the scattered islands of Polynesia. Polynesia is a huge area of the Pacific, extending from Hawaii on the north, to Easter Island off Peru to the east, and New Zealand to the southwest. Three thousand years ago people of Southeast Asia shrugged off their homelands and fled into the islands of the southwest Pacific. The sea level was lower then, the islands closer together. Living was easy along the sea shore: the ocean bounty was endless and fruit fell from the trees. To the east, though, the islands were further and further apart. Migration slowed. Technology had reached its limit.

To make the giant leap out to the far islands of Polynesia, "many islands" in Greek, new vision was needed. Voyaging canoes, which could stay at sea for months, must be designed. Food and water supplies determined. Most of all, some method of finding their way across the trackless seas, which join the many small islands together, must be found. The sea was their highway but upon it there were no signs. The voyage of discovery, of adventure, often began in a sea of tears for there was no certainty. No certainty the voyagers would find an island out there, over the horizon. No certainty that the voyagers would ever return. Too bad the many stories of heroes long disappeared in failed attempts have been lost, like the heroes.

Over the centuries the Polynesians learned. The technological changes were not easy or inspired overnight. First the canoe – double hulled would be best for stability. Twin sails assured redundant locomotion in case one sail carried away at sea. A small reed doghouse structure was constructed amidships to protect fresh water, food and plant cuttings. Stories, recited to boys at their fathers' knee, told of successes and failures, of the lure just over the horizon. The fearlessness of the watermen, who embraced the sea as their life, does not come in DNA. It comes from experience. Experience from watching shore birds and realizing that they went to sea every day to fish, but always returned home to land in the evenings. Following the birds in the evening would always lead to land. Experience from watching the clouds. The clouds did more than forecast weather - they could be a beacon for landfall. In the warm Pacific, the moist tropical trade winds had to pass over small volcanic islands. As the air rose over the low hills it cooled; as it cooled it condensed. The wayfinder far out to sea may not be able to see land, but he could see the cloud which did not move. He knew he had found an island.

The experience of watching the stars - so numerous they were fearful to count, to tempt the gods to add more. But they seemed to have patterns. While ashore, the wayfinder realized each island had its own zenith star. At sea, when the zenith star was overhead the wayfinder knew he was on the correct latitude for that island. By design the wayfinder had sailed to be well upwind of his destination. Now, zenith star overhead, he turned downwind and sailed to the island.

The more the wayfinders succeeded, the more they explored. They traded for sweet potatoes with South American Indians. They built huge stone monuments to their gods on Easter Island. They left the tropics for the 'Land of the Long White Cloud', New Zealand. Not that it was easy.

Even in the early 20th century, sailing luminaries would still find voyaging from Hawaii to the south Pacific a travail. Jack London wrote a book on his wanderings between Hawaii and Tahiti. It would, inadvertently, take him almost two months to make the trip in his sailboat. The ancients had made the same trip in 30 days. They led the world in voyaging at the time. When William of Normandy was assembling his army and crossing the English Channel in 1066, the Polynesians were sailing thousands of miles across the Pacific. Repeatedly. Voyaging between Hawaii and the Society Islands went on for centuries - thousands of Polynesians would pass over the seas. Tahitians would populate all of the Hawaiian Islands and become Tahitians no more, but Hawaiian.

And then it stopped. The route between Hawaii and Polynesia broke. Completely. For about 500 years. So abrupt and complete was the break that even the oral histories of the voyaging became muddled with time.

In 1973, the Polynesian Voyaging Society of Hawaii sought to recreate those early voyages. The PVS sought to prove, by demonstration, that their forefathers were men of vision, men of planning, men of courage. They proposed to sail from Hawaii to Tahiti, like their forefathers had done. They would prove to doubting academics and, most importantly, to themselves, that the early voyagers came with a purpose and a knowledge of the sea unparalleled in their time. They built their own voyaging canoe, the *Hokulea*, based upon drawings of 18th century Polynesian canoes rendered by western explorers. They trained their crew to sail the new craft. They were ready to prove their theory, ready to sail. But there was a problem: no wayfinder could be found in Hawaii.

The skill had been lost completely. With the abandonment of open ocean sailing for five centuries, the Hawaiians had lost the knowledge of wayfinding. Without a wayfinder it would be impossible to recreate the voyaging of the ancients, to say with authority "this is the way it was done."

Casting their net throughout the Pacific the Hawaiians found the one man who could help them: Mau Piailug. Mau was a Micronesian living as his forefathers on a small island not far from Yap. Each day he voyaged into the western Pacific in his sailing canoe, without compass or radio, still practicing the old ways of wayfinding. The PVS sent an emissary to Mau, to ask his help. But Mau was reluctant. To help the

Hawaiians was to break a great taboo, a great kapu: forbidden.

Among the old ones the skill of wayfinding was never taught to those outside the clan - it was too important, sacred. Wayfinding took them to their fishing grounds. Wayfinding took them to the other islands of their people. The skill was not to be taught to strangers.

Mau was the youngest of the extant wayfinders but he was not a young man. He knew his time was limited and it broke his heart that the young men of his islands wanted boats with powerful motors and radios. They rejected the hard old ways. They rejected wayfinding. Rather than watch wayfinding die out completely when he died Mau agreed to come to Hawaii to pass on his skills.

Mau spent a year in Hawaii learning the seas, the winds and the stars of the Southern Hemisphere. He had never sailed so far south, never viewed the foreign stars of the South Seas. In the Bishop Museum's Planetarium he bid goodbye to the constant star, the North Star. He learned the secrets of wayfinding with the Southern Cross. Finally, he was ready.

In May, 1976 Mau navigated the *Hokulea* from Maui to Tahiti using the old wayfinder skills. For almost a month they were completely out of sight of land. They had no radio, no sextant. Then, on the 28th day of the voyage the reserved and taciturn Mau turned to the crew and said: "We will see land tomorrow". The crew was stunned; they saw nothing, no signs.

As the sun rose the next morning the first of the Society Islands rolled over the horizon. The event was electrifying. Word flashed before them, spread throughout the Islands. The people of the Society Islands swarmed into Papeete, mobbed the town and poured into the harbor. Over 17,000 people, half the population of Tahiti, overwhelmed the crew of the *Hokulea*. The voyage had not only connected Hawaii to Tahiti, but also connected all of the Polynesians to their past.

Suddenly interest in the past swept over Polynesia like a tsunami. Hula clubs formed throughout the islands. Paddling groups competed in canoe races every week. In Hawaii, Hawaiian was taught and spoken again. Each group of islands throughout Polynesia developed its own voyaging canoe. A new school of wayfinders began training – a new generation learning long lost skills. The Polynesians had reached out and touched their past. They had found the swell. Corrected their course. And thanked their stars - like Mau Piailug.

Polynesian Voyaging Society's voyaging canoe *Hokule'a* at Sand Island, Honolulu

Hawaii Statehood 1959-1984

USA 20c

The *Hokule'a* was featured on a postal stamp commemorating Hawaii's statehood

The Spy

He had done his job too well. Helping to amend history he had effectively disappeared from it.

Takeo Yoshikawa. The forgotten man.

Yoshikawa, a young Japanese naval officer in the late 1930s, had volunteered for naval flight training. The navy pilots were the pride of the fleet, the loftiest profession for a young Japanese man. Then he had flunked out of flight training. A crushing defeat he felt that he had "lost face". He contemplated suicide. Sitting at home in deep depression he was contacted by the Navy with a question. Would he consider a transfer to Naval Intelligence?

Yoshikawa thought the unusual request over and answered "yes". Shortly thereafter three cartons of books appeared on his doorstep. The books were all in English. He received further orders from the Navy: "…learn English and learn all you can about America. You have one year." He did not know that he was now part of Admiral Yamamoto's grand plan: the surprise attack on Pearl Harbor.

Japan's aggressive and imperial behavior toward its neighbors in the 1930s met with disapprobation by the world community. Its invasion of China had been the final straw. Strangling economic sanctions imposed by countries such as the U.S. and Britain were crippling Japan. Its natural resource base was very limited. The militaristic Japanese government decided to seize the materials the world would not sell them. The "Greater East Asia Co-Prosperity Sphere" plan was implemented. It was war as the only prosperity contemplated by the plan was Japanese prosperity. The rest of East Asia faced slavery.

Yamamoto had only one fear in the Pacific: the U.S. fleet at Pearl Harbor in Hawaii. It was the only force capable of upsetting Japanese expansion plans. The Japanese plan envisioned its diplomats throwing an ultimatum at the feet of the U.S. government, followed immediately by an attack on the U.S. fleet at Pearl Harbor. But the plan needed details on both the U.S. fleet and its Pearl Harbor base.

After his year of learning Yoshikawa received new orders: proceed to the Japanese Consulate in Honolulu for duty as a commercial attaché. A commercial attaché's duty is to improve trade or business relationships between Japanese business and the host country. His position would be that of a minor bureaucrat, obscured in a blizzard of governmental paperwork. But his job would be that of spy.

Only Yoshikawa and the Consul General himself knew his real task. By day Yoshikawa hid in plain sight at the consulate, processing forms and maintaining a low profile. The evenings and weekends were reserved for his real task: spying. He was the typical Japanese tourist in the beautiful islands of Hawaii. He booked tours with other Japanese tourists, especially those which visited the beaches on Oahu. Yoshikawa had a close interest in beaches, particularly those which were wide, firm, and unobstructed by offshore reefs. He always had his Kodak camera with him while on tour. Completely taken by the beauty of the islands, he rented airplanes and instructed the pilots to take him on air tours of the islands. He and his Kodak. So what if they flew over military installations - he was a tourist. The Kodak film from those tours went right into the diplomatic pouch and straight back to Tokyo. It would turn into detailed maps of Pearl Harbor and other military installations on Oahu. Maps that would be found in the cockpits of Japanese bomber pilots.

He was punctilious in observing the Japanese rite of tea. Every afternoon he took tea at the Japanese tea houses in Pearl Ridge. Pearl Ridge, coincidentally, is located on the side of the Koolau Mountains, just above Pearl Harbor. Here he drank his tea and contemplated the splendid view to the south – the green sugar cane fields, the blue of the distant ocean, the vanilla sanded beaches, and the ships in the harbor. As a naval officer his first training had been recognizing ship silhouettes. He recognized the American aircraft carriers by their distinct silhouettes. Cruisers and battleships were more difficult to identify but he knew their class, armament and movement patterns. When he needed more detailed information he simply dressed as a Japanese cane cutter working in the sugar cane fields and walked right onto the bases for a closer look. One of the many Japanese in Hawaii, his disguise of being in plain sight worked perfectly.

Interestingly, Yoshikawa thought often of obtaining help. Hawaii had a huge population of immigrants with over one-third of its population being ethnic Japanese. He began vague conversations with various local Japanese people. None would fit. He found none so disaffected with their new American home that he dared broach the subject of spying. Too unreliable, he thought. Months later his chagrin would be complete - he was interned by the American government with many of these same people. He had considered them too unreliable to spy. The American government considered them too unreliable to trust.

Yoshikawa began to get a sense of the American Navy. The fleet appeared powerful but its leaders wedded to convention. On Mondays the fleet put to sea for training and exercise. By Friday it was always back. American naval officers liked to have their weekends ashore with their families. The fleet was orderly and reliable: battleships always tied up next to Ford Island; the cruisers on the far side, the auxiliary ships and submarines on the eastern side of the harbor near the dry docks.

All of this information flowed back to Tokyo via Yoshikawa's regular reports, transmitted from the Consulate. Little did Yoshikawa know but American code breakers had broken the Japanese Consulate codes. Later they would break the Japanese Navy's codes, giving the American Navy a decisive victory off Midway Island. But that was a year in the future. For now the code breakers fell into the Japanese Navy's trap. The Americans considered the consulate messages which they received low priority. They were, after all, just messages about business and trade. So the consulate messages stacked up at the code breaker's office, slowly being decoded and read. It was not until four months after the Japanese attack on Pearl Harbor that Yoshikawa's regular reports to Tokyo were read.

More is the pity as, on December 6, 1941, Yoshikawa received a secret, immediate action message from the Navy. He was to "…report immediately ships in the harbor". Yoshikawa did not know the reason for the message, only that it was an order. He immediately complied. He reported in detail the number and class of warships in Pearl Harbor as of Saturday afternoon. He repeated himself in emphasizing that the American aircraft carriers were not in the harbor. Then he went home to bed.

His world, and everyone else's, shattered early the next morning. The sound of explosions came from all over the island. Huge, thick, black smoke clouds obscured Pearl Harbor. The Japanese air attack early that Sunday morning was a complete surprise - destroying American fighter aircraft on the ground, bombing ground installations and decimating the American fleet. The blow was crushing, almost as great as Yamamoto had planned. Japanese aircraft controlled the skies over Oahu. Then, an odd thing.

The admiral commanding the fleet withdrew after only two air attacks. American forces were prostrate at his feet, but he withdrew. Yamamoto's plan was defeated by circumstances. Neither of the American aircraft carriers were in the harbor - both were at sea on separate missions. The long sword of the American navy, the aircraft carriers, had survived. Fearing an ambush by the sudden appearance of the American carriers, and content with his victory, the Japanese admiral withdrew.

Yoshikawa, and the rest of the consulate staff, awaited the inevitable. One day after the attack the FBI swept up the entire consulate staff. As diplomats they would receive immunity from any punitive action, but they would be interred on the American mainland until repatriation to Japan could be arranged. It was late in 1943 before Yoshikawa made it home to Japan. He found a very different world.

Instead of a hero's welcome for his role in the successful attack on Pearl Harbor, he found the world turned upside down. By 1943, the Japanese Empire was in retreat everywhere. Yamamoto was dead. Nobody in the Navy cared about a former spy or what happened in 1941, they were desperate to halt the retreat. The war was really over but the militarists would not admit defeat. For another bloody year and a half the war dragged on. In 1945, when the war ended and the Allies landed in Japan, Yoshikawa went into hiding. He feared retribution by the Allies for his role in the Pearl Harbor bombing. But, once again, he found nobody really cared. The world was too concerned with atom bombs and communists, rebuilding Japan and peace in Korea.

Years later he told his story. It would be treated as a minor footnote of interest only to historians. He would die an embittered man, uncelebrated by his service, unacknowledged by his country, and unremembered by history. The spy who had hidden in plain sight had disappeared.

Pearl Harbor: *Arizona* Memorial on the right, battleship *Missouri* on the left, Ford Island Airfield control tower in the center.

The Death of Cook

It had all been just a terrible mistake. Things got out of hand. It was tragic, really. An accident, a fatal one. Today, a lonely monument stands in solitary salute, isolated across a small bay, on the location of the tragic event.

James Cook was undoubtedly the most famous navigator of the 18th century. Indeed, his name is still revered as a paragon of exploration, navigation expertise, and accomplishment. He was called 'Captain Cook' but was only a lieutenant in the Royal Navy. Yet, because he commanded a ship, he was entitled to be called 'Captain'. He was not a British aristocrat nor did he have much in the way of political influence. He was a steady and accomplished British naval officer who was, at first, charged with a relatively minor task: sail to Tahiti and observe the transit of Venus.

The Royal Navy had a problem with navigation. In the 18th century, navigation was still an inexact science. The Navy paid a huge toll in shipwrecks as its ships, unsure of their exact position, piled up on both charted and uncharted reefs. Some men of science proposed that if the transit of Venus across the face of the sun could be plotted from different locations on the globe, they would be able to more accurately plot the circumference of the earth. This, in turn, would help them determine longitude. Not true, as is turns out, but the effort gained unexpected results. During his journey, Cook explored and mapped many previously unknown Polynesian islands. His scientists would bring back exciting new discoveries, titillating the world by the display of unknown floras and faunas, all magnificently exotic. Cook was sent three times to the Pacific to explore and map. His discoveries confirmed the presence of a continent called

Australia. He brought back the first maps of a place called New Zealand.

In his third voyage he was asked to do the impossible – find the mythical 'Northwest Passage'. The northern way around North America, the Northwest Passage, was the Holy Grail of exploration. The only problem was that it didn't exist. Nobody knew that for sure, so Cook was sent to confirm or deny its existence.

So Cook returned to the familiar waters of Tahiti. He spent some time refitting his two ships, *Resolution* and *Discovery*, and charting islands with their attendant bays and possible anchorages. He then departed to the north, headed for Canada and the pursuit of the Northwest Passage. However, a strange thing happened enroute. About a month north of Tahiti, land was sighted; but there was no land there. At least none plotted on Royal Navy charts. It appeared to Cook to be a series of islands - and it was. Cook and his crew were the first men to sail from Tahiti to Hawaii in over 500 years. As Cook approached the island of Kauai, canoes came out to greet him, offering fruit and fish for trade. The language that was shouted from the canoes sounded much like the Tahitian language Cook had mastered. He would constantly wonder how these people, so similar to Tahitians, had arrived in these islands over 2,000 miles from the nearest land. He would never know the answer to that riddle.

As Cook coasted around these strange islands, he arrived off the Big Island, Hawaii. His arrival was mistaken by the Hawaiian priests as the coming of the god Lono. He was treated with reverence and pomp and his two ships were loaded with fresh food. Cook and his crew ventured ashore and formed acquaintance and friendships with many of the Hawaiians. Cook's log reflected his surprise at the relative wealth and organization of this new society. There was obviously a royal court, the Ali'i, complete with king and courtiers, a priestly class, and a common people accomplished in a variety of trades. His relationship with the Hawaiians was one of mutual exploration - neither side understood the other. But the Hawaiians, a Stone Age people, understood the superior technology of the westerners and the clear implication of their metals and tools. Nothing of metal was safe around any Hawaiian. They wanted it all.

Despite the serendipitous finding of these islands, Cook was not to be deterred from his main mission of seeking the Northwest Passage. The small expedition headed north into the Pacific, the ships groaning under the gifts of food supplied by the Hawaiians, only to return. A storm at sea had sprung the main mast of one of the ships. It was foolish to continue in such condition so Cook returned to Kealakekua Bay on the Big Island for repair.

The coast of the Big Island is not the creamy sand beaches that many imagine of Hawaii. Instead, the beaches, if they exist, are black sand and rocky. Many are small with little protection from ocean waves. Kealakekua Bay offered modest protection from the ocean swell and access to forests for timber for repairs.

The Hawaiians were troubled by the return of Cook. If, as they supposed, Cook was a god, why did he return? It was not his season. He had left - he should remain gone until his time of coming next year. Why would a god need help in repairing his strange canoe? A certain uneasiness crept over the Hawaiians and their relationship with the strangers. Perhaps they weren't gods at all; perhaps they were something else? While Cook and his crew struggled ashore to find and shape a tree with which to repair their main mast, trouble broke out.

Early one morning the officer of the watch reported to Cook that one of the ship's boats was missing. The *Resolution's* two boats had been tied off behind the ship overnight. Someone had cut one of the boats loose overnight and stolen it. This was a very serious matter to the British. The boats were the only way for the crew to get ashore for water and supplies. Without his boat, Cook knew he was in serious difficulty. Cook knew he must act immediately to recover the boat.

A landing party of red-coated Marines, armed with muskets and bayonets, was ordered out. Leading the landing party, in two boats, Cook landed on the rocky beach on the north side of Kealakekua Bay. As this was the area where the Ali'i lived, he was greeted by a welcoming committee. He brushed aside the greeters and headed for the king's house. Kalaniopuu was the Ali'i nui, king of kings, of the Big Island of Hawaii. Kalaniopuu and Cook had formed a respectful friendship as Kalaniopuu recognized Cook as, if not a god, at least the Ali'i or chief of the strangers. He was honored by Cook's sudden appearance but surprised that he would appear unannounced, which was Cook's whole intent.

Cook had dealt with theft by locals in a variety of islands in his explorations. A show of force, sometimes even the use of force, had inevitably resolved the problem. Another strategy had been to seize a head man and hold him hostage against the return of the stolen item. Both methods had worked equally well for Cook. Cook intended to take Kalaniopuu on board his ship and hold him hostage for the return of the stolen boat.

Little did Cook know that his action was too late. A sub-chief had ordered the theft of the boat during the night. The boat had been hauled ashore and burned for its nails. Metal fasteners were more valuable than gold to the Hawaiians.

Cook began insisting that Kalaniopuu accompany him to his ship, immediately. Kalaniopuu was an elderly man and the Ali'i nui. He was usually sheltered by his court from this type of sudden activity. He had no wish to offend his fellow chief, Cook, by refusal but was confused as to Cook's insistence and urgency. Cook's animated behavior also alarmed the court, who urged the king not to go. The sight of the red coated Marines, with bayonets fixed, did nothing to calm the members of the court. Over the loud objections of the court Cook managed to get Kalaniopuu started down the path toward the beach. The sound of an altercation near the king's home brought other Hawaiians running to investigate. Confusion reigned. With Kalaniopuu in Cook's close company there was no one to issue orders to the court. Various commands were shouted among the Hawaiians. Some tried to block the route of march to the beach. Others gathered weapons. Pushing and shoving with the Marines began. The Marines made threatening gestures with their bayonets toward the Hawaiians. The Hawaiians were not intimidated. They knew nothing of firearms but did know they had the contingent of Marines greatly outnumbered. They demanded the release of the king. Cook refused. The beach was in sight. His boats waited just offshore. But the press of the Hawaiians was too much. Rocks were thrown. A musket fired, then another. Clubs and stone daggers appeared in the hands of the Hawaiians. Cook ordered the king released and his men to fall back to the beach. Too little, too late. By now the melee had become general, men struggling, stabbing, falling. Marines, offshore in the boats, began to fire into the crowd. Cook turned his back to the shore and began waving to his boats. Some would say it was a signal to cease firing. Others would say it was a signal to come in immediately and take them off. Much would be written about the actions of the officer in command of the boats that day. The writings would not compliment him.

Cook, on the rocky beach with his back to the shore, was struck from behind by a club. He fell to his knees. He was then stabbed with a stone dagger as he disappeared under a mass of attackers. Their leader down, their boats still offshore, the press of the Hawaiians too great, the surviving Marines dropped their muskets and swam for the boats. The struggle was over. The boats pulled for the safety of the ships, which had run out their cannon. There was nothing to do now but count the dead - on both sides.

The British were stunned by the death of their leader, a legendary man. The Hawaiians were equally stunned. What had happened? Nobody had felt ill will toward Cook. The King thought of him as a fellow leader. He admired him. The King mourned. When the King mourned, everyone mourned.

Overnight the British licked their wounds. The Hawaiians buried their dead, including Cook. Since the King regarded Cook as an Ali'i, he would be buried as an Ali'i. The Hawaiians believed that a man's spiritual power, or mana, reposed in his bones. The rest was just so much flesh. Therefore, they only buried the bones of their kings; the rest of the body was disposed with. They buried their kings in secret, their mana and their bones preserved for eternity.

Charles Clerke assumed command of the expedition. One of his first orders was to demand of the Hawaiians the body of Cook. The British wished to give their leader a proper burial. They had no idea that the Hawaiians had already done so. After much delay, the Hawaiians turned over some of Cook's bones. What happened to the rest of them will never be known. The return of the bones would give rise to an ugly rumor: the Hawaiians had not only killed Cook but eaten him too. False. The Hawaiians, and most Polynesians, were not cannibalistic. On special occasion they may have indulged in human sacrifice, but they did not eat people. Instead, they had returned to the British that part of Cook which the Hawaiians regarded as sacred. They had sent this strange Ali'i back to his people, his mana intact.

Today the lonely monument on the small bay is accessible only by foot or by boat. The foot path runs two miles downhill, and two challenging miles back uphill. One may also kayak over from the state park on the other side of the bay. It is just as the Hawaiians had accessed the bay those many years before. For a man who would have towns, rivers and islands named after him, it is small enough tribute. The monument is mournful, standing in isolation all alone. When the King mourns, everyone mourns.

Captain Cook Monument on Kealakekua Bay, Big Island of Hawai'i

Rainbow Warrior

Benign neglect would be too harsh a term to describe the French administration of the Society Islands. Taken in a coup de main by the French fleet a century and half ago, the French have refrained from pouring too much of either sweat or treasure into the islands. Still, in downtown Papeete at rush hour, there is sufficient wealth on display to cause an onerous traffic jam. On balance, the Tahitian people would probably accept less wealth if it meant less traffic. When your home, however modest, is covered by breadfruit, mango, banana and coconut trees, with the fruit falling at your feet, the quest for stock options and hedge funds seems a world away.

Many people in these widely scattered islands are little bothered by the French, in truth. Other than some modest technology, they live very much as their forefathers did. So it came as a bit of a surprise when, late in the 20th century, the French began showing interest in some of the more remote islands of the Tuamotu Archipelago, particularly an island called Mururoa. As the Society Islands had become part of the French Republic, French Polynesia, the French had assumed responsibility for their national defense, and other matters. So it was announced one day that the handful of people living on Mururoa, and nearby islands, would have to move. The islands were needed for 'special testing'. Of nuclear weapons.

The French were engaged in nothing the Americans and British had not done repeatedly in Polynesia, but that testing had ended a dozen years before. The French atmospheric testing put it at odds with governments worldwide, and environmental groups such as Greenpeace. Greenpeace was a radical group which believed in action as well as words.

They had sailed repeatedly into the French exclusion zone around Mururoa just to delay testing, increase costs and shine a public light on the radiation danger to the atmosphere. The French hated it.

Greenpeace found many had rallied to their cause. Fundraising and public opposition to the testing were both high. Late in 1984 the Greenpeace flagship, *Rainbow Warrior*, was docked in Auckland, New Zealand, giving tours, holding rallies and serving as the flagship of a small squadron of ships which planned to sail to Mururoa. The squadron would enter the exclusion zone near Mururoa, spread out and defy the French Navy to seize them all. Testing would have to be suspended until all were removed from the exclusion zone.

New Zealand was the perfect launching point for such an effort. The Kiwis had long before declared themselves "nuclear free". Even warships of friendly states could not call in New Zealand ports unless declaring that they carried no nuclear weapons.

The Greenpeace crew had been overwhelmed by their friendly reception in Auckland. Visitors swarmed the harbor and the *Rainbow Warrior*. The press expressed interest in their cause and future activities. Visitors were still crowding the ship the evening before departure to Mururoa. The crew worried about ending the festivities and preparing for the coming departure. They were needlessly concerned.

Late that evening, exhausted by entertaining and preparing for sea, the crew were all dead asleep in their cabins. The *Rainbow Warrior* suddenly gave a huge heave, almost leaping from the water. The captain thought they had been rammed by a passing ship. The chief engineer thought something in the engine room had exploded. All knew that

Rainbow Warrior was suddenly taking on water, listing and starting to sink. Everyone scrambled for the dock. The Greenpeace photographer, Fernando Pereira, suddenly realized all of his cameras and film were below in his cabin. He raced below to rescue them from the salt water. As he did so *Rainbow Warrior* gave another huge heave and settled to the bottom. He died in his cabin.

Auckland woke the next morning to stunning news. Not only had there been a tragedy to the Greenpeace ship and a death, but the police investigation was more concerning. *Rainbow Warrior* had two man-sized holes in her side. Her steel plate was pealed inward, as if by a bomb. What could cause such holes? It could only be a military type weapon, placed professionally next to the engine room below the water line. How many people have both the tools and the training for such an effort?

The Kiwi police overcame their surprise to focus on motive and opportunity. They issued a nationwide bulletin for constables to be on the alert for unusual activity by French nationals within New Zealand. The next day, a rental car company at the Auckland airport phoned to say a French couple had turned in their car a week early. They were suddenly leaving New Zealand. The police interviewed the couple. Their papers were found to be 'irregular' and they were detained. They stated they had been staying in a travel trailer during their holiday in New Zealand. It was parked next to the Auckland Harbor. The police searched the trailer and found sophisticated scuba gear inside it. When the trailer's floor boards were swabbed, the swabs tested positive for explosive residue. The couple was arrested and charged with murder and arson.

Meanwhile a park ranger on the far end of North Island had called in. He reported speaking with four young Frenchmen who had arrived at his park by sailboat the week before. They had come in from New Caledonia, French territory, on holiday. They had promised to clear customs the next day but had never appeared. They had been seen leaving the park in a travel trailer, towed by a vehicle occupied by a French couple. When the police arrived, the sailboat had already left the park bound for New Caledonia.

When the sailboat called at Norfolk Island, the Australian police detained the crew. The New Zealand police flew up to interview the four men. All admitted landing in New Zealand, but they were merely on holiday. The police were allowed to swab the floor boards of the sailboat but had no way to test their swabs. The boat and its crew were released by the Australian police as they had no warrant to make an arrest. The sailboat disappeared to the north and was never seen again. Meanwhile, back in New Zealand, the police test of the swabs from the sailboat was positive for explosive residue.

Investigation of the French couple in custody indicated that their passports were false. They were not a couple at all. They were two French military officers: Major Alain Mafart and Captaine Dominique Prieur. When this fact was announced to the press, the story became global.

Maddeningly short of facts the press hounded both the New Zealand and French governments. Both remained mum but the press remained on high alert – the story had too many elements that pointed to scandal. When the New Zealand prosecutor announced both French officers would be tried for murder and arson, the French government objected loudly. Nevertheless, to court they went.

On the day of the trial the courtroom was packed by the world press. Auckland had never bathed in the glare of so much press attention. Starved for information the press knew that as the trial unwound the facts would come out. But the trial unwound too fast. The defense immediately announced to the judge that the defendants had accepted a plea bargain offered by the prosecutor. They pled guilty to the lesser charge of manslaughter. The press went wild – they had been cheated out of their story. More was to come. The judge had not been a party to the agreement and plea bargain. The judge now had to pass sentence, and since he regarded even the lesser charge as a serious offense, he sentenced the defendants to ten years in prison. It was the French government's turn to go wild. Apparently they had expected some sort of probation for the crimes, but the judge disagreed. The defendants were swept off to prison. The French government retaliated.

Suddenly, New Zealand lamb could not be imported into French Polynesia or New Caledonia. Then the bombshell landed. The French government introduced a bill to the EU Parliament to forbid the import of all New Zealand agriculture products into the EU. The war of words heated up. The New Zealand Prime Minister called the *Rainbow Warrior* incident "…a sordid act of international state-backed terrorism" and laid the responsibility directly at the feet of the French President, Mitterrand. The French government denied all. The confrontation between the governments deepened. Finally the U.N. Secretary General stepped in to broker a peace. The French officers would be turned over to the French military to serve out their sentences on a small French military base in French Polynesia. In return, the French agreed to drop all boycotts of New Zealand products.

Unfortunately, after six months incarceration in French Polynesia, Major Alain Mafart developed a serious stomach ailment which could only be treated in Paris. He was flown home for treatment. He never returned to complete his sentence. Equally unfortunate, Captaine Dominique Prieur developed a slight case of pregnancy. Her husband had been allowed to accompany her in her incarceration. Since the French military base had no medical facilities to care for a pregnant woman, she was also flown home to Paris. She never returned to complete her sentence.

But the press, especially the French press, knew a good story and a scandal when they saw one. The story just would not die in the Paris newspapers. Plus, small leaks oozed out of the military and the government, continually stirring the pot. Whispers of "Mitterrand approved" continued to circulate in Paris. The sailors who had disappeared on the sailboat bound for New Caledonia reappeared later, in Paris. They were special operations members of the French Navy.

Finally, in an attempt to end the speculation, the French Defense Minister resigned. The French admiral in charge of special operations took early retirement. The whispers continued. When the Mitterrand government finally fell, the new government had no compunction about answering the press' questions. It admitted the *Rainbow Warrior* event had been a special military operation approved at the highest levels of the French government.

Peace finally came between France and New Zealand, but at a price. The price was $30,000,000 in reparations and expenses for the New Zealand investigations and trial. Greenpeace would net $8,000,000 from the French, enough to buy a new ship. And the old *Rainbow Warrior?* Even though she was damaged too badly to ever go to sea again, she did, in fact, go to sea. Towed from the Auckland harbor she was sunk just outside to form an artificial reef, home for both sea life and scuba divers. She rests there still. And Mururoa? Like other island victims in paradise, it rests deserted – forgotten by the French, forbidden to its people.

Greenpeace's *Rainbow Warrior* rests on the bottom of Auckland Harbor after being sabotaged by French commandos.
Photo courtesy of Te Papa Museum, Wellington, N.Z.

Battery Randolph

Poi, they say, is an acquired taste. Hawaiians love it, but many westerners find it bland, more like paste. Oh, it can still be purchased at mainstream restaurants, such as the Shore Bird on Waikiki Beach. But it's not a big seller in the tourist markets.

Poi, of course, is a paste. Made from the baked root of the taro plant, it has been a staple of the local diet since Hawaiians arrived from Tahiti about 1,000 years ago. Each Hawaiian home in antiquity had a poi pounding board and pedestal shaped tool to pound the taro root. Water was mixed with the pounded root and pounding continued, along with the addition of water, until the poi reached the proper consistency. It could be one finger, two finger, or three finger poi, the consistency determining the number of fingers needed to eat it. It was served as a starch, much like westerners ate potatoes or pasta.

Waikiki was the perfect place to grow taro. The taro plant required a swampy, watery environment. As rain water from the Koolau Mountains cascaded down the south side of the hills into the Waikiki area it stagnated, forming low, wet country. Here the Hawaiians had established huge taro patches, cultivating the root for poi for centuries.

By the beginning of the 20th century, the United States had annexed Hawaii as a territory. Hawaii was a necessary stepping stone out to the American colony of the Philippines. It was also a defensive bastion to help protect what would become the Panama Canal. Pearl Harbor, just west of the Honolulu Harbor, was considered the perfect anchorage for the American Navy. But the southern shore of Oahu would require some type of defense from foreign invasion or attack. The taro fields would have to go.

The Army needed not only land to house its troops in forts, but also land upon which to build coastal defense batteries. At the beginning of the 20th century, the airplane as a weapon was still a remote idea. Military planners still thought in 19th century terms viewing attack by a large enemy surface fleet as the prime threat. Coastal defense batteries of large caliber cannon, similar to those guarding the entrance to San Francisco Harbor, must be built. But where?

Honolulu, at the beginning of the 20th century, was not the bustling metropolis it is today, but it was no small village either. Exclusive hotels had sprung up downtown on Waikiki Beach. Plus, Hawaiian royalty owned quite a bit of Waikiki. Nobody wanted to live next to a fort full of soldiers, nor a defense battery which might be shooting off large guns. The low, swampy taro fields beckoned.

A wealthy Honolulu businessman named Chun Afong owned three acres right on the beach in western Waikiki. His villa was the site of many nightly gatherings, watering the elite, the influential, the wealthy. Army officers were invited to these soirees. They eyed the location with its southern exposure. Perfectly placed cannon here could guard the entrances to both Honolulu Harbor and Pearl Harbor. They made Afong an offer he couldn't refuse. Afong had not become the first Chinese millionaire in Hawaii by turning down lucrative deals. He sold the villa to the Army for $28,000.

The taro fields came next. What had been a swamp would, of course, serve our Army perfectly well. The Army bought the land but fooled everyone. They converted the low, swampy fields into a parade ground, office buildings, and quarters. They called it Fort DeRussy. DeRussy had been an Army general and head of the Army's Corps of Engineers. But, more interestingly, he had invented the Barbette Depressing Gun. This gun was styled a "disappearing gun". This huge coastal defense gun was mounted on a telescoping mount which raised and lowered the gun. The idea was to construct a solid, thick concrete wall in front of the gun. When the gun needed to fire it was raised over the wall, fired, then lowered behind the wall for reloading. The wall would protect the gun and its crew from counter-battery fire from enemy ships.

Fort DeRussy would have its own battery of "disappearing guns". Right on the beach at Fort DeRussy the Army built Battery Randolph, followed later by Battery Dudley. Battery Randolph would be huge and mount two guns which could, just in themselves, serve as a deterrent. Any attacker faced 14 inch rifles which could hurl a 1,560 pound shell up to 14 miles. Any ship, no matter how large, getting stung by these guns would be, indeed, hurt.

Battery Randolph would hide behind 12 foot thick steel-reinforced concrete walls. Its guns would pop over the walls, lash the enemy and drop back into its protection for reloading. The battery would require four dozen artillerymen just to service the two guns. Almost as an afterthought, Battery Dudley, next door, would be equipped with two six inch guns - relative pea shooters to Randolph's guns.

Of course any gun which can hurl almost a ton of steel over a dozen miles must have a powerful propellant charge. Randolph's guns did. When the battery was completed in 1914, the Army warned all of Honolulu that the guns would be test fired. Nobody listened. The morning the guns fired, the concussion kicked the crockery out of China cabinets all over town. Windows rattled and cracked. The uproar by the citizenry of Honolulu was almost as loud as the guns. The Army agreed that it would not test the guns too often. And it did not.

Fort DeRussy and Battery Randolph would continue to guard the southern coast of Oahu for years. The coming of the airplane as an instrument of war would require Battery Randolph to adopt a steel reinforced concrete roof for protection from aerial bombardment. The roof would be just as formidable as the reinforced walls surrounding the battery.

On that fateful day, December 7, 1941, with the Japanese attack on U.S. forces in Hawaii, the Army knew it must be ready for anything. Battery Randolph would test fire again. Honolulu, by this time, had grown into a thriving tourist town. Despite adequate warning when the battery fired windows at hotels up and down the beach shattered. Hoteliers could only imagine what a battle would do to their properties.

Fortunately, the war ended with the battery never being used. By 1946, the idea of coastal defense batteries was obsolete; airplanes would guard the coast in the future. Therefore, the guns of Dudley and Randolph were likewise obsolete. In that postwar world, the guns were sold for scrap metal. The batteries closed, being used occasionally by the Army as warehouses. The facilities at Fort DeRussy fell into disuse until only a dilapidated officer's club on the beach and a base chapel were all that was left.

Twenty years later, the Vietnam War saw an upswing in military activity in Hawaii. Hawaii served as a way station for troops going to and coming from war. The military determined it needed an R&R facility, rest and recreation, for its troops, and Hawaii was perfectly placed. Fort DeRussy, on the beach with its unused facility, would do nicely. The old buildings would be torn down and new facilities constructed. The wrecking ball was called in.

The military's idea of clearing out the old fort structure, opening the Fort DeRussy area as a beach park, was brilliant. They had another brilliant idea in that a hotel was needed. The Hale Koa Hotel, "House of the Warrior", would be built on Fort DeRussy property to provide affordable accommodations to service men in Honolulu. There was only one problem. The problem's name was Battery Randolph.

To prevent any hint of inappropriate use of taxpayer money, the military decided to build the hotel using only recreation funds, which are funds raised from military recreation activities worldwide. The Corps of Engineers would supervise the hotel's construction and plans were drawn. But Battery Randolph, standing right on the beach, was in the way. Send the wrecking ball. As with the taro fields, Battery Randolph would have to go.

Contracts were let and the demolition contractor moved in. The crane was raised, wrecking ball rigged out, and hundreds gathered to say goodbye to the 19th century. The wrecking ball swung back and then hurtled toward the battery's walls. It bounced off. Withdrawn, reswung, it bounced off again. And again. No matter how many times it swung at the battery wall the battery wall got the best of it. Some crumbled concrete lay on the ground but the battery stood defiantly. Not to be outdone by an obsolete building constructed with 19th century ideas, the contractor moved to another part of the battery and tried again. Same result. They tried again, at a new location. Same result. Battery Randolph, built to withstand the shells of battleships, was not about to surrender to a mere wrecking ball. The contractor battered the battery right into bankruptcy, and the battery was still standing.

Not one to give up, the Corps of Engineers stepped back and scratched its collective head. While the Corps admired its ancestors for their commitment to construction competence, the modern men were as equally determined to succeed as their progenitors had been. Explosives, and a lot of it, appeared to be the answer. Until they looked around. True, they were on a federal military reservation and could do as they pleased, but they were now surrounded by high rise hotels filled with thousands of taxpayers. What would an explosion powerful enough to undermine Battery Randolph do to those high rise hotels?

The Corps rethought. Could the hotel site be changed and Battery Randolph used for something else? Yes and no. Plans were redrawn and the hotel moved to the west side of the property. And Battery Randolph? Anyone need a building with 12 foot walls able to withstand anything?

The Army solved its own problem. Some bright lad decided if they couldn't destroy Battery Randolph they should salute it as an example of Army resolution. So it was turned into a museum: the U.S. Army Museum of Hawaii. In 1976, its dedication saluted not only Hawaiian history, but also the military's history in Hawaii and the great struggle of the Pacific war in the 1940s. The Museum is housed inside of Battery Randolph's 12 foot walls, which keep it not only cool inside, but also safe. From everything.

Fort DeRussy is still a military reservation today. One would hardly know. It is, for all purposes, the second largest public park in Waikiki. Its green lawns and wide, shady banyan trees are open to all. The occasional military policeman on foot patrol is one of the few clues to its military life. The taro fields are gone, though. But standing in the southeast corner is a large brown two story building. Out front by the street it says "Museum", but on its wall the sign still says, defiantly, "Battery Randolph".

Battery 'A', 16th Coastal Artillery pose for a unit picture in 1931. Note man in muzzle of the 14" gun.

Comparison drawing of one of Battery Randolph's guns versus a standard 7" artillery piece.
U.S. Army Museum, Fort DeRussy, Hawai'i

The Mediterranean

Pharaoh's Dream

The first boom, when we heard it, was rather muffled. We definitely heard the frying of the fuse prior to the second, more dramatic, explosion. As the MS *Noordam* stood down the Bosporus Strait heading into the Sea of Marmara, my wife, leaning on the promenade deck's rail, said to me: "Did you see all those people?"

Istanbul, as they say, is an interesting place. Of course any place with 3,000 years of history is an interesting place. One thing is certain: with that much history, there has certainly been change. In the late spring of 2013 we didn't realize we would witness part of it: "…all those people" she was referring to were the start of two weeks of explosive demonstrations against the Turkish Prime Minister, Recep Erdogan. More secular, and younger, Turks were protesting his turn to the right and what they perceived as infringements on their freedoms. So they took to the streets. The demonstrations turned into civil disobedience, complete with tear gas, police confrontations, personal courage, and governmental denouncements. But this boom would pale compared to our next destination: Egypt.

Travel time from the port in Alexandria to Cairo is almost three hours. We found the travel guide on our bus to be young, educated, and chatty. She told us all about Egypt: pharaohs, the Pyramids (to which we were traveling), the countryside (desert), and the people. On our return trip she had run out of history so she turned to current events. It became clear, in an unmistakable way, that she, and many like her, disapproved of President Morsi's governance of Egypt. As a litany of Egypt's problems spilled forth from her mouth they could be confirmed by a glance out the window of our bus. She spoke of a petition, signed by millions, which would be presented to Morsi the next week. They hoped for change. Little did they know how much change they would get. Thousands exploded into riot, the government fell, Morsi was jailed, the military, once again, took over. This boom would be heard all over the world. Not the first time for Egypt, though.

Egypt. Birthplace of civilization. Certainly land of many riddles. It is also a land of such wealth that conquerors for thousands of years would covet it. The pharaohs had ruled for a thousand years before Alexander brought his great army. Caesar did fall not to the armies of Egypt, but to the arms of Cleopatra. Crusaders landed, bent upon conquest of the Holy Land from the land of plenty. Napoleon saw it as a key to victory and a greater empire. French engineers saw it as a great, historic opportunity to build a grand canal. But they were several thousand years late with the idea.

The Nile has always been the source of Egypt's wealth. Gathering water and force as it flows down from its birthplace in the mountains of central Africa, the Nile is the beating heart of Egypt. Its great annual floods, spreading wide in its river valley, not only watered the arid land but spread new top soils to nourish the crops. It also served as a highway through Egypt and its deserts. The Nile dhows, with their lateen sails, are emblematic of the Nile, as are the caravans winding along the banks of their watery lifeline.

The Nile also served as the highway of trade from the exotic east: India, the Spice Islands, and that far away mystic, China. Across the Indian Ocean and up the Red Sea the spices and exotic goods flowed, only to be stopped at the marshy area of Suez. Here the cargos were unloaded onto caravans for transport across the desert to the Nile, thence down the Nile to Alexandria, trading port of the Mediterranean. Would it not be faster and cheaper if the cargos could be floated over to the Nile? Could not a canal be constructed from the Nile to the Red Sea?

History from 4,000 years ago is dim and misty. But the idea of a canal obviously was an idea with long legs, which would stand the test of time. It appears that Senausret III, fifth ruler of the Twelfth Dynasty of the Middle Kingdom, employed canals around 1878 BC to move his troops. He built a canal around the first cataract of the Nile, and he toyed with the idea of a canal from the Nile to the Red Sea. Was he the first to build such a canal, or does the credit go to Sity I in 1310 BC? In any event, some monarch caused a canal to be built from one of the lower Nile distributaries probably to the Bitter Lakes region. One can only imagine the back breaking work with pick and shovel in the desert to build such a structure. It would rival the Pyramids in effort; only Pyramids don't sand up, which was the fate of most of the early canals.

Necho II, however, was a man of ambition. Expansive in view and aggressive by nature, he not only was a conqueror but a builder. Around 600 BC, Necho commanded that a canal would be built from the eastern-most distributary of the Nile to the Red Sea. He was so sure of his success that he had a new city, near modern Ismailia, built. Being the monarch of one of the world's richest countries means unlimited resources. Well, almost unlimited. According to Roman historian Herodotus, Necho stopped work after 120,000 slaves had perished in his attempt. Herodotus says "....Nechos, then, stopped working on the canal and turned to war." His neighbors were restless and Necho was ruthless. He would not be the first ruler to find out that guns and butter at the same time was an expensive proposition. Necho preferred fighting to building.

Time marched on and so did the conquerors. One hundred years after Necho it was the turn of the great Persian, Darius I. Darius the Great, he would call himself. Persia, today, we also know as Iran. Darius conquered Egypt as part of his plan of world domination. He, also, reviewed the advantages of having a canal link to the Nile from the Red Sea. He ordered it done. Some historical sources, such as Strabo and Pliny the Elder, would avow that he did not conclude this work. But we now have it, stone-faced, that he succeeded.

During the construction of the current Suez Canal four stone stelas, or stone monuments, were discovered. Kings loved erecting stone stelas which would record their accomplishments for eternity. In this case, Darius' record has stood for only 2,500 years. On his stela Darius had inscribed: "I am Darius. I am a Persian. From Persia I conquered Egypt. I ordered this canal dug from the River Nile, which flows in Egypt, to the sea which borders Persia. Thereupon this canal was dug, as I ordered, and ships sailed from Egypt to Persia through this canal, as it had been my wish." Obviously, if Darius had stelas built for the event, he considered it a significant achievement. And it was. The canal was wide enough for two triremes to pass each other and took four days to navigate. The dream of water borne commerce between the heart of

Egypt and the East was fulfilled. Almost. There was a problem.

During half the year, the Nile rose in flood. During the other half, the Nile dropped to low water. When the water level in the river was low, the water level in the canal was insufficient to allow even small ships to sail. So the canal was only usable about half of the year. The rest of the year the shifting sands of the desert tried desperately to reclaim it.

Over 200 years later, Ptolemy II thought he had a better idea. Ptolemy's family was Greek. His father was one of Alexander's lieutenants. The Ptolemys' claim to Egypt came as their share of the spoils when Alexander's empire was carved up after his death. Ptolemy II brought in Greek engineers to study the problem of the canal. It was their idea to install a lock to help control the level of the water in the canal. The lock was successful enough to be mentioned by Siculus, but, once again, the canal fell into disuse.

Then came the Romans, those prodigious builders. In all probability the Egyptians, to this time, had simply continued the efforts of their predecessors in attempting the canal. The canal branched off the Pelusian distributary of the Nile. It snaked along the Wadi Tumilat, a former river bed of the Nile. It joined the Bitter Lakes at some point, piggybacking on those waters to aid its journey southward. The fact that a canal of any nature had been built at all was truly amazing, given the technologies and difficulties, but something had to be done about the low water problem. The Romans paused and rethought the problem.

If the distributary system they were using did not have enough water at the canal mouth, why not move the canal mouth where there was more water? The decision was made to move the canal mouth 60 kilometers south, or further upstream. Here, the Nile had not yet bifurcated. The full force of the river was available. The Romans dug in at the direction of the Emperor Trajan, noted for his many building projects. They dug a new western half of the canal from the new canal mouth to join the old Pharaoh's Canal around the Wadi Tumilat. From there, they simply improved the Pharaoh's Canal.

Being practical military men, they realized that a canal was not only important for trade, but also provided a rapid method of moving troops and warships. Such a liquid highway needed to be guarded. A fort was constructed at the Nile mouth, and the town which grew up around it would be known as Babylon. Later the name changed to Cairo.

Sea level elevation at the mouth of the canal at Cairo was 19 meters. Elevation at its exit point at the Bitter Lakes was about five meters. This gave the canal a gradual fall of 14 meters, over 45 feet, from entry to exit, perfect for water flow eastbound. When opened, the canal worked just as the Roman engineers had expected. Trade and troops both flowed up and down the canal, in season. The canal still had too little water during the spring in the low water months. During the spring the canal was closed and maintenance was conducted, but the Romans could not engineer around Mother Nature. As fate, or Mother Nature, would have it, when the Nile was high and the canal open, the monsoon winds of the Arabian Sea and Indian Ocean were unfavorable for a voyage to India.

It appeared that the Roman Canal would not further trade with the East, but it was still usable for Trajan's purpose: expansion of Roman power into the Red Sea and Arabia. One of the last gasps of the Roman Empire was its move into Felix Arabia: 'Fortunate Arabia'. Its use of the Red Sea linked it with Sheba, or Saba, in Arabia and opened a window into northeastern Africa. The Roman Canal appears to have been in use for over 400 years; its flat bottomed boats serving as lighters between the ocean going vessels of the Red Sea and the river dhows of the Nile. As with all things Roman, it gradually fell into disuse. For transportation it was on pause, but it still served as an important supply of fresh water for irrigation and communities of the region.

Around the year AD 643, the canal would reappear. Amr Ibn al-As had conquered Egypt for the glory of Islam and the Caliph Umr in Medina. The Caliph wrote to the general, telling of famine in Mecca and ordering him to send food as quickly as possible. Always a thinking man, al-As replied to his lord that:

"You know that before Islam, ships used to come to us carrying traders of the people of Egypt. When we conquered Egypt that canal was cut, having been blocked off and the traders had abandoned it."

The Caliph quickly authorized the re-excavation of the canal. While canal boats could not carry more grain than a camel caravan, the boats could move the grain to Arabia in a third of the time of a caravan. Trade resumed at a brisk pace, and then stopped just as suddenly for the same reason: politics. In 755 AD the Caliph, al-Mansur, ordered the canal blocked. Rebels were in control of Mecca. In an effort to choke off the rebellion, literally, the Caliph sought to starve the rebels by cutting off their food supply from Egypt via the canal. He succeeded in both putting down the rebellion and ending the life of the canal.

In 1798, the French Directorate, in control of France after the Revolution, sent Napoleon Bonaparte to Egypt. His orders, in addition to seizing Egypt and destroying British trading posts on the Red Sea, required that he "…shall have the Isthmus of Suez cut…" and take control of the Red Sea. It was a tall order even for a military genius, but a task worthy of keeping Napoleon, with his grandiose dreams and popular support, busy outside of France.

In 1799, after successfully investing Egypt, Napoleon sent his engineer, Le Pere, to begin making studies for the construction of the canal. Today, we understand that Le Pere told Napoleon that the work was impossible. He had measured the elevations of the Red Sea and the Mediterranean and found the Red Sea to be 30 feet higher than the Mediterranean. Cutting such a canal would empty the Red Sea into the Mediterranean causing disaster of unprecedented proportions.

Now we must pause and consider Napoleon's true dilemma. He was faced with building a hugely expensive canal in the midst of an expensive war with Britain. And the canal would join two seas which were indisputably controlled by the Royal Navy, which could be counted upon to oppose every French move. Impossible it was, but not for the stated reason. The French had been building canals for centuries. The Midi Canal in the south of France had been in use over 100 years at the time of Napoleon's campaign. French engineers well understood the use of locks to balance variances in terrain, but it was an effective excuse to abandon a millstone project.

Strangely enough, it would be French engineers who would reawaken the project in the middle of the next century. Not the Pharaoh's Canal or the Roman Canal, but the canal we know today as the Suez Canal. This canal would ignore the Nile and be cut directly from the Mediterranean at Port Said through the Bitter Lakes to the Gulf of Suez on the south. Digging in the desert is thirsty work, fresh water would have to be brought in from somewhere. What better place than the Nile? A "sweet water" canal would be cut from the Nile to parallel part of the main canal. Once the sweet water canal was cut, the main work of digging the Suez Canal could begin. And the route? From Cairo on the Nile, along the Wadi Tumilat to parallel the proposed main canal to the Bitter Lakes. The engineers of the modern would find they were walking, literally, in the footsteps of the engineers of the ancients. While the sweet water canal was a considerable engineering feat, it was even more of an archeological feat. It excavated many remnants of the Pharaoh's and Romans' Canal, proving, once again, that the history of mankind over the centuries is not so different now than it was then.

Today, the canal linking the world at Suez is a foregone conclusion for transportation and trade. Huge ships, which would frighten the Pharaohs, and maybe even the Romans, ply the canal. It links world economies and is the viaduct for the transport of vital supplies to nations. Its shortcut drives profits, creates industry, and supports the region. Just as the Pharaohs had dreamed, 4,000 years ago.

Suez Canal north of the Bitter Lakes.

Father

I don't think about my Father much anymore. He's been gone a long time now. And when he was with us he led a quiet life. I think that he believed that he had earned that quiet in 1944. In a post office.

Still, one cannot cruise down the coast of Italy without reflecting upon famous names. There is Pompeii with its attendant drama of eruption and terror; Capri with the aura of wealth, fame and glamour. Other names evoke other images today. Anzio: a fierce battle characterized by poor generalship on our side. My Father's regiment landed at Anzio. When he talked of the war, which was seldom, he always referred to Italy as "It-lee". He spoke once of being in reserve at the battle of Monte Casino. Mostly my family remembered "It-lee" by the cameos he had brought home to my Mother.

It is the same with the south of France. There is something about the light there that brought the impressionist artists and inspired their work. The south of France brought more than artists, though - it brought money. The famous and the rich have their villas, occupied only in the summer, carved from the cliffs of France's southern and scenic coastline. My Father never mentioned once his cruise from the coast of "It-lee" to the south of France, where his regiment was, once again, tossed onto a hostile beach. I suspect his cruise was considerably different from his son's. The only ones sniping at us today are the vendors on the pier when we fail to buy.

My Father was a postman by trade. Not the kind that stuffs letters into your mailbox at your home. That guy is a letter carrier. My Father was a postal clerk, who sorted the mail at the main post office and gave it to the carrier for delivery. It was a secure job that he had won during the Great

Depression and he was not about to give it up, even in the Army.

The Army. What an operation. In 1942 they had tried to draft my Father four times but turned him down all four times. He kept flunking his physical – flat feet. So, fifth time around they took him. Naturally, with flat feet, they assigned him to the infantry. He went off to Fort Robinson in Arkansas for training, my Mother trailing behind. After almost a year they put him on a ship. All they told him was 'destination Europe'. Older than most of the draftees of the day, he had been promoted to buck sergeant before leaving the U.S. He was a combat infantryman, and a postal clerk. We still have the photo, taken while at training, of him in full combat gear, bayonet fixed and in the 'on guard' stance, ready to impale the enemy. That was not the man I knew.

Normandy, on the northwest coast of France, has assumed a pilgrimage status for many. People come from all over the world to see the landing beaches of D-Day. All one has to do is walk along those beaches, then called Omaha and Utah, gaze over the dunes and up the cliffs to decide instantly that being on those beaches in June 1944, was a very dicey business. True, the Normandy landings came first. But the landings in the south of France, long forgotten, were not unopposed. Those were Germans behind those guns.

My Father never saw himself as a "doughboy". It was a word which was supposed to have gone out of style with the end of World War I. Some members of the press kept calling our GIs "doughs" or "doughboys". That isn't how our soldiers saw themselves. My Father purchased a copy of Bill Mauldin's book *Up Front.* He carried that book with him. My Father always liked Mauldin because, as a newsman, Mauldin was there, he was with them. He portrayed the life of the GI as it was. My Father always preferred the moniker of "dog face", which Mauldin had hung on the common soldier. It was a dog's life: few comforts, constant danger, fatigue, poor food, bad officers. My Father didn't particularly like officers. He never said why, but the truth would ooze out of his voice whenever he said the word "officer".

His regiment had pushed far enough north by December 1944, that they had been sent to a rest camp for a break and refitting. By this time he was a staff sergeant and in charge of the regimental post office. Mail was a huge morale item for the troops, probably as important as decent food. That December morning they were busy in the post office sorting the mail. The rest camp was located close to the French/German border. As he told the story "some officer" came into the post office and announced: "The post office is closed. Get your weapons and get up on the line. There's a bulge in the line."

Yep. They were headed for the Battle of the Bulge. He never told his children the story, but he told my cousin. And my Mother, some of it, anyhow. My cousin liked to tell the story of how my Father's company was crossing a large field and the Germans opened up on them with a machine gun. They all dove for cover. The only cover my Father could find to hide behind was a head of cabbage growing in the field. He would later say "...it was not much cover". My Mother's favorite story, which she would tell us kids, was how my Father's regiment was relieving another outfit during the December battle. As they were moving into the line the Germans started to shell them. My Father ran for a fox hole, planning to dive head first into it, to escape the shelling. As he neared the fox hole, he saw that the fox hole was full of water and the water had a skim of ice on the top of it. It was mid-December in Europe; the ground was covered in snow and the temperature had been below freezing for weeks. As she told it, he realized that if he dove into the fox hole he would be soaked in freezing water and may die of exposure before he could dry out. If he didn't dive in he may get killed by the shelling. She always liked to stop there with a smile on her face. As I grew older I became impatient with this story and its lack of ending. Finally I asked her, "Well, what did he do?" She looked at me with a bit of surprised expression on her face and paused. Finally she said, "I don't know, but whatever it was it must have been right because he's here with us."

That was the answer. Whatever it was it was the right thing. He morphed from a postman to a squad leader, leading men into combat, sending others to their death. The Bulge Battle over, he continued as part of the Rhineland Campaign, a bitter and bloody contest, the dying gasps of a monster. Later, his outfit linked up with the Russians at the Elbe River in eastern Germany, which would become East Germany. He transferred to Military Government and became the acting First Sergeant in a small occupying force in a town east of the Elbe. The Russians kicked them out. Powerful forces in Washington ordered all U.S. troops back across the Elbe. East Germany was going to become Communist, but not before one last confrontation. As his outfit, departing for the west, approached the Elbe River bridge, they were stopped by a Russian road block complete with machine guns. As the unit stopped, the Russians insisted on searching its trucks. The captain in command said something akin to "over my dead body, nobody is searching our trucks without orders". They sat there all day, eyeball to eyeball with the Russian roadblock. Finally, at sunset, the Russians told the captain he could leave. No search. My Father said he was proud of "that officer".

He had earned his peace, in 1944, and again in 1945. He's at rest now, lying beside my Mother. At his feet is a simple bronze plaque. All it says is: "Paul Eschenfelder, Staff Sergeant, WWII, American Expeditionary Force – Italy, France, Germany". We were proud of him. We are proud of him.

Private Eschenfelder assumes the *en garde* stance, preparing to defend his nation. (left)

Staff sergeant Eschenfelder is all smiles after having survived the Battle of the Bulge and the Rhineland Campaign (right)

Marathon Man

Most people, unless they are an orthopedic surgeon or athlete, are completely unaware that they possess an IT band. My wife was certainly unaware as she was training for the Shell Houston Marathon. Since she was "only" going to attempt a half marathon, a mere 13.1 miles, she was unconcerned with overtraining, to her sorrow.

The whole story came back to her as we stood at the entrance to Panathenaic Stadium in downtown Athens. The Greeks had done an excellent job of modernizing the old stadium for the 2004 Olympics, where it served as the finish line for the Olympic Marathon. One can only reflect with chagrin, as the runners crossed the line, that athletes had been competing at this location since 330 BC. But the first Marathon sprint had a different purpose altogether.

The IT band is a mass of fibrous tissue which runs from the hip down over the knee to stabilize the knee during running and jumping. Too much running and jumping can cause swelling and irritation of the IT band, so much so that the orthopedist, who held my wife's knee in one hand and ankle in the other, simply shook his head "no". No race for her. While she was crushed to be pulled from the race so close the event, she fared far better than Pheidippides, the original Marathon man.

The root of the Marathon began in a Greek town by the name of, well, Marathon. Located about 25 miles north of Athens it is only a few miles from the Gulf of Marathon, separated from the Gulf by the Plain of, well, Marathon. A historic site. Strange, isn't it, that this place, known now for a race, also had a hand in the birth of modern democracy?

About 500 BC, a great ruler emerged in Persia. He styled himself Darius the Great. He was certainly great at military victories and consolidating his power. Ruling an area from the borders of India to Egypt, across the Dardanelles into modern Greece and through the Balkans, he wanted more. Naturally, the local people were unimpressed being forced under his boot heel, but none had the power to stop him. He seemed invincible, he seemed Great.

Darius' army had swept over Asia Minor, modern Turkey, overwhelming the Greek city states along the coast. The Persians then piled into modern Greece, conquering some city states, forcing others into subservience as vassals. Only Athens and Sparta were strong enough to resist, and to aid in the resistance of others. When some of the Greek cities in Asia Minor revolted, Athens sent an army to aid them. The Greeks burned the Persian town of Sardis. Darius was furious. He vowed revenge. He vowed that he would burn Athens. He instructed a servant to whisper to him every night as he sat down to dinner: "Remember the Athenians". Darius' fire of revenge burned brightly, indeed.

Darius gathered a great army, sending it on a mission of conquest and destruction to quench his fire of revenge. They were first to recover the rebel Greek cities, then conquer those Greek isles not yet in their possession, and, finally, burn Athens to the ground. The army advanced with great anticipation and success. The Greek rebels were crushed. The Cyclades were invaded and seized. Now it was the time to destroy Athens.

If one regards a map of the region, it is easy to see why the Persians proceeded to Marathon. From Delos in the Cyclades it is an easy sail, in protected waters, almost due north to the beach at Marathon. The Persian army was huge, estimated between 20,000 and 40,000 men, so it required a huge navy to transport it. Such a large number of ships required quite a large beach for landing, to discharge both infantry and cavalry. The cavalry was the pride of the Persians. Able to move rapidly and strike swiftly it was the prime reason the Persians had been so successful. While the Persian infantry confronted the enemy, forcing them to engage head on, the cavalry galloped swiftly to the enemy's rear and struck from behind. Forced to fight on two fronts, and usually unprepared for the rear attack, the enemy frequently broke and ran, always an invitation to slaughter.

Not only did such a large army need a large beach upon which to land, it required a large area in which to camp. The Plain of Marathon fit the bill perfectly. It helped that a deposed Athenian tyrant, Hippias, was advising the Persians, showing them the way to Athens and the recovery of his throne, he hoped. Not everyone in Greece at the time was a believer in democracy. Tyranny would do fine, provided you were the tyrant.

The Athenians were of another view. This new experiment of democracy was a messy business, but they discovered it gave them certain freedoms and improved the life of the common man. They liked it well enough to fight for it. They particularly did not want to give up their freedoms to a distant ruler of a foreign culture.

The Greek army was an interesting group. Formed mostly of citizen-soldiers who had received some basic military training, they were primarily interested in completing the battle and returning to their homes and businesses, such as farming. A short war was important to the stability of the economy. These citizen-soldiers were known as hoplites, a reference to the round shield they carried. Unlike other armies, the hoplites were armored to some degree. They wore a bronze helmet, bronze chest protector, and bronze leg guards. Most carried a large round shield and a spear. In combat they formed into close ranks, known as a phalanx, and advanced or fought shoulder to shoulder, shields up and interlocking, spear tips forward. It was a fearsome group to attack.

The Persians found that the Plain of Marathon was bounded by high hills to the north and swampy low lands near the beach. They also discovered that the road south to Athens was, unfortunately, blocked by an Athenian army. Upon learning of the Persian landing near Marathon, the hoplite army had formed up, moved out swiftly, and blocked the only passage from the beach to Athens. Here they stayed. For days.

Each army eyed the other across the open plain. Each looked for an advantage, a mistake by the enemy. The Athenians played for time. They knew they did not have enough troops to engage the large Persian army. They needed to send a swift runner to Sparta to ask for the help of the Spartans. It was over 120 miles to Sparta, and 120 miles back to Marathon. Pheidippides was chosen. Reputed to be Athens' best long distance runner he covered the distance from Athens to Sparta in two days. And, incredibly, from Sparta to the army's location at Marathon in a like two days. The news wasn't good.

The Spartans were coming, but not soon. They wanted to help the Athenians but were in the middle of a religious period and could not leave Sparta until the full moon, six days hence. The Athenian generals counseled. It seemed unlikely that the Persian army would stand still for over a week. As it was, the Athenians had them bottled up on the beach. But if they embarked and sailed away, they could land anywhere and regain the advantage. Plus, there was that unfortunate point of being outnumbered by at least two to one. The Athenians equivocated.

Miltiades, one of the Athenian generals, stepped forward. He made an impassioned speech to the army's leadership, reminding them that they were fighting for the future of democracy, the future of Athens. They had to secure the future and there was only way to do so: defeat the Persians.

The other generals agreed. They appointed Miltiades as commander of the army. Miltiades ordered the Athenian army to form up, shoulder to shoulder. Since the Persian army was so large and strung out across such a broad front, he ordered the center of the Athenian phalanx thinned and moved troops to both flanks. This act would prove Miltiades either an extremely brilliant general or an extremely lucky one. He then ordered the army to advance.

The Persians could not believe their eyes. They had a huge and decisive superiority in forces. Their army was formed up in battle order. For the Greeks to attack them was not only unexpected, it was tantamount to suicide. However, the Persian commanders missed two points which Miltiades grasped.

First, the Persian cavalry was missing from the field. In the haze of distant history, no one can adequately explain where the cavalry had gone. The best guess is that the

Persians had decided to move to another location more favorable to them. In that case, the horses would be embarked first as they took the longest to load. So there would be no swift counterattack in the Greek rear by the fast moving cavalry. It would be a straight infantry battle, soldier against soldier.

Second, the Greek hoplite armor was far superior to anything the Persians wore. The Persians counted on a shower of arrows from their bowmen to decimate enemy forces on their advance. Then the infantry would overwhelm the survivors. The Greek armor gave Miltiades another idea.

The Greeks advanced in perfect formation of the phalanx for over a mile. But at a point 200 yards from the Persian lines, the beginning of arrow range, the entire Greek army broke into a dead run directly at the Persians. Imagine, a full sprint of 200 yards wearing 70 pounds of armor, then a hand-to-hand fight at the end of the run. Words like 'athletic' can't describe such men. The Persians found the Greeks were covering the kill zone of the arrows too fast, plus the arrows were bouncing off the shields and armor of the Greeks. The Greek army struck the Persian lines intact and at full speed. The weight of the superior Persian numbers kept their line from collapsing and the battle was on.

There was little room for maneuver by either army on the Plain of Marathon. The armies had filled the Plain and were essentially pinned into the center of the Plain by the hills and swamps on the sides. It became a battle of the numbers, where superior forces would tell. The center of the Greek line, thinned by Miltiades, began to slowly give way under the force of the Persians. As the Greeks retreated in the center, the Persian center advanced, causing a large bulge in the Greek line. As the Greeks retreated further more and more Persians poured into the bulge. Then the heavy flanks of the Greek line, which had won their fight, began to slowly rotate toward the center, joining together and cutting off the Persian center. The Persians in the center suddenly saw that they were being cut off and would be slaughtered. The Persians sensed the trap closing and broke ranks. They began to run for the beach. Once an ancient army broke ranks while still in contact with the enemy, the rout was on.

As thousands of Persians fled back to the beach and the safety of their ships, they found their ships had already put to sea. True, the Persian navy was now too far out to be seized by the Greeks, who would only capture seven ships of the great fleet, but it was also too far out for their own troops to reach. They had been abandoned on the beach. The Persians ran for the swamps with the Greeks in full pursuit. Mercy and surrender were on no one's mind. The slaughter was great.

Herodotus, the Roman historian, said that the Persians lost over 6,000 men that day. The Greek loss was 192. It seemed a clear victory, but the danger was not yet over. Greek scouts, following the Persian fleet, saw the Persians turn west around Cape Sounion. That meant that they were headed for Athens for an attack from the west. Here, myth merges with reality. Pheidippides would emerge again after only 500 years.

Miltiades understood the threat to Athens. He rested the army overnight and then began a forced march the 25 miles back to Athens. The army arrived on a promontory west of Athens in time to watch the Persians, once again, unload from their ships. As the Persians formed their army, again, they found their way to Athens, once again, blocked by the Athenian army. Exactly what went through the Persian commander's mind is unknown. After a day of staring at the Athenian army, he ordered his army to re-embark and sailed away. Athens was safe. For now.

Yet the story of Pheidippides would run on through history. Undeniably, he had completed a great run to Sparta and back, but myth would create a greater role for him. According to tradition, after the Greek victory at Marathon, he was sent on a sprint to Athens to carry the news. The legend has him sprinting the 25 miles from Marathon to Athens to announce to the government "Rejoice, victory!" before dropping dead at the leaders' feet. This story does not gain legs until 500 years after the battle. It runs even harder in more modern times where he is celebrated by poets and sculptors.

Unfortunately, the story is unlikely. A man who could run 250 miles in four days would be a poor candidate to expire after a 25 mile run. More so, if the news of the battle had been bad, there was nothing Athens could do to defend itself. It had been virtually stripped of able bodied men to man the army. Plus, victory on the Plain of Marathon did not guarantee safety; the Persian fleet was still at sea. Yet the story does cast a heroic image, and a legend was born.

With the birth of the modern Olympics in Athens in 1896, an event celebrating Greek history was suggested. The English poet Robert Browning had, only 19 years before, written a poem celebrating Pheidippides and his faux run. The poem achieved wide circulation and was on the minds of the Olympic Committee. So a 'marathon' run from Marathon to Athens was added. This race was only 24.8 miles and run over the course Pheidippides supposedly ran. The 1908 London Olympics would change all that. The Royal Family wanted to observe the start of the race from Windsor Castle, so the race was extended to accommodate them. This made the race 26.2 miles from Windsor Castle to the predetermined finish line in London. So it stands today: 26.2 miles.

What stands today, also, is the fact that anyone who can run 26.2 miles must be an Olympian. Also, no matter what course he had run, Pheidippides was a champion. Oh yes, and the Greek victory at Marathon? It had opened a window to allow the experiment called democracy to sprout and grow. Messy business that it is, democracy had its first flower at Marathon.

Modern statue of Pheidippides in Syntagma Square, downtown Athens

St. Mark's Bones

She was the typical blushing bride with an endless smile and a glowing aura. Italian, her dark complexion was offset by the brilliance of her long and amazingly white wedding gown. Lace flowed down the gown, overlaying and offsetting the silky dress. She daintily and effortlessly held up her gown, just far enough so that the mud brown hem of the dress revealed her rubber knee boots. No matter, she and her party waited with anticipation. Their wooden hulled water taxi, which was attempting to tie up, was golden with its many coats of lacquer, its refined Chris Craft lines threatening to out dazzle the bride, at least in a yachtsman's view.

The bridesmaids were not fairing so well. Their pink gowns dragged in the muddy water as they scrambled to aid the bride down the board walkways of St. Mark's Square. The sirens had sounded, the warnings had gone out and the water had come up. Venice, which makes its living on the Lagoon, fell victim again to "acqua alta", a usual hazard of the fall. A series of high tides and northerly winds, which prevent the earlier tides from draining from the Lagoon, stack the water up into flood stage in the town. But no matter. The city places elevated wooden walkways over the main calles, and pedestrians bold enough to attempt them simply carry on. Tourists, who don't understand the broadcast warnings, need look no further than just inside the main entrance of their hotel. The lineup of rubber boots should be warning enough.

The high water meant little to the wedding party. The bride and her attendants scrambled into their water taxi for the short ride across the Grand Canal to the grandest day of her life, soon to unfold at the Basilica di Santa Maria della Salute. Life, in Venice, unfolds as it has for a thousand years.

Today, the uniqueness of Venice makes it seem as if it has been with us forever, similar to the eternal city, Rome. Rome, however, was old when Venice struggled into existence.

Both the apostles Paul and Peter were busy at work in Rome when Venice was still regarded as a magnificent place to hunt ducks and to fish. Few structures existed in the Lagoon and its appeal was only to sportsmen. On the other hand, further north along the coast of the Adriatic was the wealthy town of Aquileia. Aquileia had an interesting patrimony.

For a member of the Roman legion the greatest hope was to live until retirement age. Upon retirement Rome would provide for the retired soldier. Unlike today's military retirees, who receive a monthly stipend from their government, Rome's soldiers were more likely to receive a grant of land which they could farm, supporting themselves and perhaps selling any surplus. After years in the Legion it was a true Fiddler's Green life for the retiree.

The land gifted was usually in a frontier – unclaimed land which could also serve Rome as a buffer. Aquileia was such a place. Its town site was on a large abyssal plain on the very north of the Adriatic, but it was on a key pathway into northern Italy from the Balkans and eastern Europe. Any visitors, or invaders, must pass this way. Starting life as a military post Aquileia had grown as more retirees moved into the area and commerce boomed. It had everything the citizens could want, except one thing: Christianity. The locals appealed to Rome for an ecclesiastic leader.

When the Apostle Peter had left Jerusalem, he had done so in a hurry. Herod Antipas had thrown him into prison and was planning his execution. Fortuitous intervention by an angel had sprung him from his cell. Peter had hit the road and had swept up the disciple Mark on his way out of town. As a simple fisherman Peter had no knowledge of Greek or Latin. Mark, a well-traveled and well educated disciple, would serve as his interpreter and scribe for years in a variety of cities and, finally, Rome. When the request came from Aquileia, Peter knew that Mark was the man for the job.

Mark's work in Aquileia was a great success, planting a large church and winning many converts. He sought to return to Rome but decided to name an eminent local man, Ermagoras, as bishop. To do so, he would need Peter's blessing. Both embarked in a boat and set out along the lagoon's canals for Ravenna, thence overland to Rome. While passing through the Venetian Lagoon a high wind arose, causing them to tie up overnight on one of the islands in the Lagoon. During the night Mark had a vision. In his vision an angel appeared, which prophesized that a great city would be built on that location to honor his evangelical efforts. The next day the duo continued their journey to Rome, where Ermagoras was, indeed, confirmed as bishop of Aquileia.

There is little doubt that Mark was an evangelist. He had worked with Peter on the road, been his right hand in Rome, written the Gospel of Mark and itinerated in Aquileia. Now he was called to Alexandria, the great port city of Egypt. Alexandria was the second most important city in the Roman Empire and probably the wealthiest. It was the meeting place of the world - where the Orient met Europe. Goods flowed from India and China up the Red Sea, overland to the Nile and down to Alexandria. At Alexandria, all of Europe bought and sold. Whatever enmities between races, countries, beliefs existed, all were suspended in Alexandria in favor of trade. Mingling here were Romans, Greeks, Jews, Egyptians, Arabs, Persians, all with their own religions. It was truly a melting pot and, for a Christian evangelist, a huge opportunity, but one fraught with peril.

Mark met with the local Christian community and then began boldly preaching the Gospel in public places. He began to win a large number of converts, and a large number of enemies. Any new idea, whether religion or politics, is upsetting to the established order. Religious leaders of all stripes lined up against Mark and his Gospel. When he could not be persuaded from his public proselytizing, the decision was made to simply eliminate him.

Forewarned of the plot, Mark left Alexandria in charge of his first convert, Anianus. He sojourned for several years in various cities of North Africa, spreading the gospel. Upon his return to Alexandria he found the Church much strengthened and larger. He ordered that a new church be built in eastern Alexandria and that church stands today as St. Mark's Cathedral. He also became known as "the exterminator of idols". This did not bode well for him.

Leaders of those sects whose idols Mark assailed banded together. All knew that Mark would be in Alexandria for Easter and where to find him. On Easter morning a mob formed and armed itself. The mob flooded into Mark's church as he was celebrating Easter Mass, put a rope around his neck and dragged him from the church. They then dragged him by the neck mercilessly through the streets of Alexandria. Finally they threw him into a prison cell, unattended. Overnight, his injuries proved too much for him and he expired.

Rejoicing, his enemies sought to erase all trace of Mark by casting his body onto a large funeral pyre. As the fire was started a violent thunderstorm passed over, drowning the fire. His tormentors fled the storm and his disciples were able to rescue his body. He was interred in a crypt under his church. There he lay, peacefully, for about 700 years.

Now we have one of those interesting episodes of history in which each side tells the same story, differently. By the year AD 828, Egypt was under the control of Muslims. While Muslims had no particular desire to persecute Christians, neither did they feel any affinity for them. A great building campaign was underway in Egypt as the Caliph had decreed that more and better mosques were required. Building materials were needed and what better place to look for them than in current buildings, such as churches. This caused much worry among the Christians. Rumors circulated throughout Alexandria that the Muslims would tear down churches to use their building materials. Anything within the church would be destroyed, including Mark's bones.

Relics of the saints and all things holy had taken on a life of their own in the Middle Ages. Relics were venerated and worshiped - the objects of pilgrimages and prayers. The worship of relics became so widespread that in AD 787, the Seventh Council of Nicaea decreed that every consecrated altar must contain some type of relic. Not to mention the fact that the possession of a relic of one of the disciples of Christ, or one of the four evangelists, was a serious political statement for a city. Such possession would give a city not only prestige, but bragging rights that it was more powerful because it was favored with a saint's remains.

By the ninth century Venetians were at sea and practicing a burgeoning trade. They would not become a trading giant for several hundred more years, but they were already recognized as shrewd traders. Several Venetian ships were in Alexandria during this troublesome time for Christians. Two Venetians, Bono from Malamocco and Rustico from Torcello, sensed either a duty or an opportunity. With turmoil roiling the Christian community of Alexandria, they went to St. Mark's Cathedral. Here they met with the monk Staurazio and the priest Theodore, who were the custodians of the sanctuary. Over a period of several days they convinced Staurazio and Theodore that the proper and safe thing to do with Saint Mark's bones was to allow them to transport the relics to Venice for safe keeping. When the Muslim troubles were over, Mark could be returned, or so the story goes.

In any event it was agreed that the Venetians could remove Mark's bones. But this could not be done in secret. Word leaked out that Mark's grave was being robbed - a large angry crowd gathered in the Cathedral. The mood turned ugly as the crowd loudly demanded that Mark remain in peace where he was buried. A hasty assurance flew from the lips of all the conspirators that everything was right - Mark's bones were intact in his crypt. Look, see for yourself. Except those weren't Mark's bones. As the mob had gathered, the diggers hastily opened another crypt and placed another's bones into Mark's empty crypt. Mark's bones were hidden in a wicker basket next to the Venetians.

Even when the Venetians had spirited the basket back to their ship, they were not out of the woods, so to speak. The port's customs inspectors were sure to search the ship, seizing any untaxed items. A basket full of bones was bound to arouse suspicion and investigation, something to be avoided. The Venetians filled Mark's basket, and several other wicker baskets, with cabbage leaves layered with cooked pork. When the Muslim inspectors asked what was in the basket the answer came back: "Kanzir, kanzir". Pig. Anathema to a Muslim. There was no search of the baskets.

The date of Saint Mark's arrival in Venice is still celebrated: January 31, 828. Bono and Rustico tendered the bones to Venice's leader: Doge Particiaco. All of Venice marveled and cried. The Doge decreed that a church worthy of the Saint should be erected next to the new Doge's Palace. Four years later Mark would be put to rest, again, in the new chapel called San Marco, Saint Mark's.

It would not take four years for Venice to adopt Mark as its patron saint, however. Mark was a powerful saint and his symbol was that of the lion, a perfect fit for the aggressive Venetian psyche. The old patron saint of Venice, Saint Theodore, was jettisoned in favor of Mark. Theodore had been a Byzantine saint, anyhow, plus he had no relics. Mark was the perfect fit. Soon the symbol of Venice, the winged lion, spread throughout the Adriatic and then the Mediterranean. In his paw the winged lion holds the book on which is inscribed "Pax tibi Marce evangelista meus": peace be with you, Mark my evangelist. These are the same words reputedly said to

Mark by the angel in the Venetian Lagoon 700 years earlier. So the ancient prophecy had come true, or at least as true as the Venetians could make it.

Mark was not one to rest peacefully. Two hundred years later, a fire would decimate his chapel. When the chapel was rebuilt in 1094 as the present Basilica, Mark's bones were nowhere to be found. The entire city wept and prayed. The Doge proclaimed a fast for the whole population until Mark's bones were found. Then, according to legend, Mark extended his arm from a pillar of the new basilica, indicating the location of his bones. The Doge and Bishop had him re-interred, amid great ceremony, under the high altar where he has remained since.

The Venetian people had high hopes for their new Republic. It could be that one saint simply wasn't enough for them, or it could be that the theft of Mark's bones simply inspired others. So much so that in 1100 AD, Venetians would spirit away the bones of Saint Nicholas from his resting place in Myra, in Asia Minor. Nicholas was the patron saint of sailors and merchants, a perfect description of the Venetians. When it was rumored that sailors from Bari had beaten them to the crypt and already removed the relics, the Venetians retorted that the Bari sailors had removed the wrong body and had left Saint Nicholas in his crypt. They instead had taken possession of Nicholas' relics, venerated them and moved them to Venice. A new church was built on the Lido, San Nicolo, the church of the sailors. There Nicholas lies today, his divine protection reaching out to all at sea.

Building a legitimate legacy and demonstrating superior spirituality was thirsty work for the new Republic. Two saints were good. Three would be even better. The

Venetians went back to the well. Aiding Christian forces during the Crusades, the fleet of Doge Domenico Michiel veered off course and raided the Greek island of Cephalonia in 1124. They seem to have forgotten that Greece was part of the Byzantine Empire, a Christian state. There they looted the bones of Saint Donatus, carrying them back to Venice. Donatus was reputed to have slain a large dragon in Cephalonia and the dragon bones were whisked away also. Today they hang behind the altar of the church Santi Maria e Donato on Murano for all to see. The saint is interred above the high altar, behind the dragon bones. The only problem is no one is quite sure which Saint Donatus the Venetians had grabbed. There was a Saint Donatus of Arezzo, an Italian saint. He was well traveled but seems out of place in Greece. Then there was a Saint Donatus of Albania, said to be interred in Corfu, a Venetian possession. No matter, a saint is a saint for relic purposes.

As for Saint Zechariah and Saint Athanasius, both were swept up by the Venetians. Zechariah was said to be father of John the Baptist. His remains had been removed from Jerusalem to Constantinople by the Byzantines in the early days, venerated in the Hagia Sophia. However, the Fourth Crusade, during the sack of Constantinople in 1204, stripped everything of value out of the city. Much of it went to Venice, including Zechariah's bones.

Athanasius was a later day bishop of Alexandria. How his bones came to Venice, one can only imagine. But their authenticity was vouchsafed by Pope Paul VI when he returned part of the relics to the Coptic Church in Cairo in 1973. Here the Venetians scored a two-fer. Both saints are interred in a double-decker shrine in the Church of San Zaccaria, not far from St. Mark's Square.

If the presence of holy relics rendered prestige and power, then Venice would be behind only Rome itself in authority. A city, a republic, bent not only on success but on unbounded success, would stop at nothing. Indeed, that would be a criticism of the Venetians. It was no coincidence that Shakespeare would write the *Merchant of Venice,* and not the Merchant of London or the Merchant of Rome. The Venetians earned their reputation. They were unparalleled sailors, shrewd merchants, and men of dubious conscience. But that is a story for another day.

The Bride wears boots to her wedding at the Santa Maria della Salute on the Grand Canal

Residents and tourists alike brave Venice's "acqua alta" waters.

One Onion

Mykonos has not always been an island for the rich and famous. Sleepy Greek fishing village that it was, it changed because of the paparazzi. It seems they were successful in tracking Jackie O to Mykonos on one of her vacations to leave the world behind.

Mykonos, at the time, was certainly a place to do that. Little changed over time, it was still a small village of narrow alleyways, cats, pelicans, and windmills. The island's many small beaches, adorning small coves, lent privacy to the beach goers. And, if you had your own yacht, the mild weather and beautiful water provided all a visitor needed.

But, as with any trend setter, the discovery that Jackie Onassis holidayed in Mykonos changed all that. So much so that today cruise ships, tying up at the new piers on the far side of the harbor, discharge waves of tourists who, at times, threaten to flood the town. Fortunately, the town is well prepared. The narrow alleyways are lined with jewelry store, shoe shop, jewelry store, shoe shop, all at the visitor's disposal. Tired of shopping? The many tavernas provide respite. A little confused as to exactly where you are in those narrow alleys? The locals tell the colorful story that the alleys were built narrow and winding to confuse pirates, a plague in earlier days. The truth is much harsher. It centers on a man named Barbarossa.

Piracy, of course, has been with us since man first learned to steal. When man learned to sail he simply took stealing to sea. It's a human failing, one still with us today, but never done on such a scale as the days of Barbarossa.

Actually there were two Barbarossas; they were brothers. The elder was much more impetuous than his younger brother, given to great adventures and great risk. Eventually, as with all poor risk management, he could no longer defy the odds and came to a bad end at the hands of the Spanish. However, we are getting ahead of ourselves.

In the Middle Ages the Mediterrean was a very different place. Although rulers could claim vast empires they could not, in effect, command them. The further from the seat of power the territory lay, the more independent the local ruler became. Communication was poor, if at all, and allegiances shifted continually. The "pax romana" of the Romans was gone - only the strong, or clever, survived.

By the 15th century, the Mediterranean had been, again, recast. In 1492, the Spanish had completed the "Reconquista", or the reconquest of all of the Iberian Peninsula, wresting it from the Muslims, or Moors. Spanish policies pushed all Moors, regardless of their allegiance, out of Spain. Their lands and property seized, the Moors arrived in northern Africa penniless and bitter. This invective contributed a hard edge to what was to follow.

As elsewhere in the world the Mediterranean suffered with piracy. There were Greek pirates, Arab pirates, Venetian pirates, Muslim pirates, Christian pirates in the Knights of Malta. Pirates of every stripe. Rulers of the port cities along the North African coast not only tolerated pirates, they tacitly encouraged piracy. It was a sweet deal: in return for providing only a safe harbor for the pirates, the local ruler shared anywhere from one-eighth to one-third of the booty, at no risk to him. Should a powerful European monarch object, the Bey would simply shrug and say "What can I do, they are pirates."

Piracy, however, was at a fairly low level. A successful pirate leader may have only a handful of ships which followed him – powerful enough to overcome helpless merchant ships, but smart enough to fly in the face of military force. This was an annoyance to be sure but not a threat to empire. It was, however, a bogeyman to frighten recalcitrant children who lived along the coast. No one wanted to be seized by the pirates and sold at the slave auction in North Africa. Death would be better.

Enter the 16th century, and enter the Barbarossa brothers, Oruch and Hizir. Refugees from internal strife in the Ottoman Empire, they arrived in North Africa with only two traits: an intimate knowledge of seamanship and a bad attitude. It did not take the elder brother, Oruch, long to determine that piracy against Christian shipping was a calling at which he was extremely adept. The growth of his small pirate fleet and some of his audacious captures brought him to the attention of the Sultan of Tunis. For a modest fee, only one-fifth of the take, the Sultan offered him the shelter of the Tunis harbor and a market for his purloined goods and slaves. It was a refuge the brothers welcomed. In it they prospered and grew bold. Pickings were easy and Barbarossa's reputation for cruelty ran ahead of him, so much so that some ships he attacked gave up without a fight.

Tunis was well located for a pirate. Here, the great bulge of the African shore shoulders north into the Mediterranean. The Sea necks down and its travelers must squeeze between the great shoulder and the rock of history, Sicily. Sicily, like Sardinia, the Balearic Islands and the southern half of the Italian peninsula, were all the domain of Charles V, King of Spain and Emperor of the Hapsburg Empire, a most Christian ruler. A ruler whose territory and people would provide not only the wealth of the Barbarossa brothers, but their very reason for existence.

Oruch, known as Barbarossa or "red beard", was a man of boundless ambition, optimism, and cruelty. He wanted more than a pirate lair: he wanted a kingdom. His successes at sea would serve him poorly on land. Several times he assaulted the small Spanish garrisons along the North Africa coast. These garrisons, woefully undermanned and poorly supplied, were meant to be the symbol and strength of Spain on the African coast. Instead, their occupiers viewed them as the ends of the earth. As one Spanish officer said: "In the New World there is gold and jewels; here there are only Turks and Moors." Barbarossa repeatedly threw himself against these garrisons and failed, even leaving pieces of himself behind.

In 1516, a new opportunity arose. The Arabs in Algiers were pinned in their city by the Spanish who were holding the harbor's fort. They, to their regret, asked for Barbarossa's help in expelling the Spanish. Barbarossa entered Algiers to much fanfare – a hero to their rescue. He promptly strangled the Sultan in his bath and declared himself ruler. His 16 galleys and thousand pirates made the title secure. He was now lord of most of Algeria.

Algiers was practically on the doorstep of Spain. Charles would not tolerate a pirate as aggressive and evil as Barbarossa in possession of Algiers with its great harbor and strong fort. He sent a huge force, over 10,000 men, to Algeria to wipe out the pirates. Oruch, a hundred miles inland seeking to consolidate his title, was cut off from the sea. His flight from fate was desperate - he even scattered gold and jewels on his trail to distract his pursuers. It was not to be. Cornered in a wadi, his violent career came to a violent end. His head and cloak were sent back to Spain as living proof that the pirate of legends was dead. The Spanish then went home.

Yet they left another Barbarossa behind: Hizir. The younger brother was every bit as aggressive as Oruch, but much more prudent. The title of leader of the pirate bands now devolved to him. When the Spanish failed to follow up on their victory by attacking Algiers, Hizir made a shrewd move. He knew, alone, he could not stand against the might of the West. He sent an emissary to Selim, Sultan of the Ottoman Turks, in Istanbul. He offered his loyalty and his lands as a vassal of the Ottoman Empire. Rarely has one man gained so much by becoming a servant.

Selim was busy consolidating his conquest of Egypt. But here, on a plate for virtually nothing, came a major expansion of his empire. Selim accepted the offer. To Hizir he sent more than just the horsetail banner of Governor General of Algeria. Selim also sent a dozen Turkish galleys carrying 2,000 Janissaries, the cream of Turkish troops. And a new title: henceforth Hizir Barbarossa would be known as Hayrettin – "Defender of the Faith".

Hayrettin Barbarossa lost no time changing life in the western Mediterranean. He attacked the Spanish garrisons along the Algerian coast and took possession of each of them. He launched his 18 galleys on an annual voyage throughout the western Mediterranean islands and along the Spanish coast. The pirate fleet not only snapped up helpless merchant vessels, but also stormed ashore throughout the region, looting villages and carrying away Christians by the hundreds to the slave market in Algiers.

Barbarossa kidnapped on a grand scale. Kidnapping was good business, one which had no downside for the pirate. Wealthy people could be ransomed. Those without wealth or influence were simply sold at the slave market. Workers were always needed in the fields, at day-labor in the towns, or as galley slaves to pull on the Moors' oars for the rest of their short and unfortunate lives. A galley slave had nothing to look forward to but a brutal life, chained to his bench and only to leave it when he was cast overboard when no longer able to row. As Barbarossa's fleet increased in size, he needed more and more slaves to man his oars. It was incongruous to many that Christian slaves provided the power for the galleys of Muslim terror. As Barbarossa's success and fame spread, he had no difficulty attracting crews from the Moriscos recently arrived from Spain, seeking both work and revenge. Soon he was surrounded by 40 pirate captains of whom the Christians would say there was no heart in any of them.

It seemed all that Barbarossa did prospered, much to the chagrin and distress of the Christians. In 1519, a large Spanish force was sent against him at Algiers. They tempted fate by sailing late in the season. When the Spanish were only half ashore, a large storm struck sending many of their ships crashing on the rocks. The army struggled ashore half drowned - only to be slaughtered piecemeal by the outnumbered Turks. All the Moors could see that Allah was on Hayrettin Barbarossa's side. For almost a decade Barbarossa sailed the

Mediterranean as if it were his own lake. Few opposed him and then only carefully.

That would change. Charles had been busy elsewhere in his empire, turning aside revolts in the Netherlands, invasions by the Turks, war with the French, and heresies by the new Protestants. He now found an ally at sea. Andrea Doria, the pride of Genoa, was probably the most famous man afloat in the era. He had sailed for Francis of France until Charles had defeated the French and marginalized Francis. Doria saw no future with a vanquished king. When Charles offered him a huge salary and the position of grand admiral, Doria was happy to switch sides. Doria had tacitly left Barbarossa alone previously. The Turks were enemies of the Spanish, the French were at war with the Spanish, and Doria worked for the French. Enemy of my enemy is my friend. No more. Charles wanted Barbarossa eliminated and peace restored to the Mediterranean. Charles sent Andrea Doria to raid the Ottoman coast of the Adriatic. He would show the Turks that the Mediterranean was Spanish, not Ottoman. It was a big mistake.

By now Suleiman had succeeded to the Ottoman throne. Known in the West as Suleiman the Magnificent, he was also known as Suleiman the Shrewd. He knew the Turks lacked experience at sea; they were people of the Steppes. Suleiman was outraged by Doria's raid against Ottoman holdings in the Adriatic. He summoned Barbarossa to Istanbul.

With cannons firing salutes, flags waving, and cymbals crashing, Barbarossa and his small fleet sailed up the Golden Horn in answer to the summons from his lord. He marched at the head of a triumphant parade of exotic animals, expensive gifts, and Christian slaves to pay homage to his master, Suleiman. In return, Suleiman appointed him *kapudan-i-derya,* grand admiral of the Mediterranean fleet. He also made him governor-general of the new Province of the Archipelago, and he turned him loose in the Turkish shipyard. If there was anything Barbarossa knew better than piracy, it was shipbuilding. Suleiman would not have to wait long for his revenge on Charles.

Barbarossa had sailed into the Golden Horn with a fleet of 18 ships. He would leave the next spring as admiral of over 80 ships. Many of these new galleys held over 100 fighting men. It was a magnificent sight as the fleet sailed out of the Bosporus. However, the reports of the huge fleet in the letters of the Western spies were enough to freeze a ruler's heart. Where were they going? News of Barbarossa's fleet spread faster than wildfire and more terror than the plague. There was nothing in the West that could stop him.

Speed was Barbarossa's ally and secrecy his weapon. He ignored the Greek archipelago and the fortified towns of the Adriatic. He swept around the toe of Italy and hit southern Italy like a sledgehammer. This was no hit and run - it was possession and destruction. Charles' soldiers ran from the pirate fleet and Barbarossa's men marched miles inland to loot and kidnap. When he entered the Bay of Naples, people in Rome, 60 miles away, began to flee. Having laid waste to the Italian coast and taken over 11,000 captives, he turned south. The new slaves went to Istanbul as tribute to Suleiman. Barbarossa went to his real objective: Tunis. This was no longer mere piracy. This was war.

With Tunis in his grasp, the Ottoman Empire would rule virtually all of northern Africa - the entire southern rim of the Mediterranean. The Maghreb would be theirs. As Barbarossa's sea of galleys bore down on Tunis, the Sultan of Tunis fled by the back gate. He wouldn't be gone long. Barbarossa set about immediately strengthening Tunis' outer fort, La Goleta, and reinforcing the town's walls using the 10,000 Christian slaves held in Tunis. He worked all winter.

Unfortunately for him, Barbarossa underestimated the Spanish reaction. Charles recognized the clear threat to his empire. Fear and religious fervor were the greatest allies on his side and he played them like trump cards. The call for retribution and revenge against the infidel Turks went out all over the Mediterranean. The Pope sent his fleet and the Knights of St. John their great galley. From Genoa came Andrea Doria with his galleys filled with troops from Germany. The Portuguese sent caravels and Charles threw in men and ships from across his empire. Most of Christendom had risen against Barbarossa. Charles would personally lead the assault. It was now Barbarossa's turn to flee.

With the summer came Charles' great fleet. When Barbarossa saw the sea turn white with its sails, he knew his hold on Tunis had little chance. It turned into no chance when renegades within his walls began freeing the 10,000 slaves. Caught between two fires, Barbarossa fled down the coast to his galleys hidden in small coves. While all of the Christian forces celebrated for days the bloody victory in Tunis, Barbarossa sailed away. To spoil the celebration.

The defeat of Barbarossa and the re-capture of Tunis was a huge weight lifted from the people of the Mediterranean. The terror of the Muslim pirates and their bloody-minded leader had been vanquished. They celebrated far and wide. They celebrated for weeks. They celebrated too soon. On the Balearic island of Minorca the people of Mahon held a festival on the town square, near the waterfront. They were even more joyous when a dozen Spanish galleys entered the narrow harbor. The people threw open their arms and bid the newcomers to join the celebration. But, instead, the galleys opened fire and hundreds of pirates swarmed over the square. Barbarossa had disguised his ships as Spanish and invited himself to the party. He burned the town and left with 6,000 captives for the slave market at Algiers. The slave market became so overcrowded that a Christian slave could be had for the price of one onion.

Barbarossa was simply demonstrating to both Suleiman and Charles that his defeat at Tunis had not cooled his ardor. He returned to Istanbul and the ship yards. The next year, 1536, he sailed again, this time with 120 ships. His goal was the complete subjugation of the Greek archipelago and the humiliation of the Venetians. He flooded over the Venetian-held Greek islands and their trading posts, completely depopulating most. He landed on Mykonos and seized practically the entire population. A lucky few escaped. No matter, he returned the next year and seized the survivors. Mykonos lay silent and empty for 40 years. Strangely, it stirred back to life as a pirate lair, perfectly located for their needs.

The pattern was now set for life around the Mediterranean. Barbarossa did not invent piracy or kidnapping, but he elevated it to a high art form and successful business model. Over the next century, the number of Christian captives dragged from their ship or their shore to the slave markets of the Maghreb numbered over a million. With western monarchs busy with more weighty matters, pirate leaders trained at Barbarossa's knee sailed virtually at will.

Residents of the Mediterranean shores learned to 'fear the horizon'. For 300 years they never knew when the sails of terror would appear, heading for their village. Rulers were forced to change the manner in which they built their strongholds. Villages were redesigned with narrow alleys and choke points where a few could hold off many, for a while. Finally, in the 17th and 18th centuries, whole stretches of coastline, particularly in Italy, became deserted. People simply moved inland. As Italian writer Piero Ottoni put it: "We retired to the countryside. We lost our freedom and our love of the sea." The nation which had produced heroic navigators now feared the sea. The memories lingered into the 20th century. As one modern Sicilian mother recalled: "The oldest [still] tell of a time in which the Turks arrived in Sicily every day. They came down in the thousands from their galleys and you can imagine what happened! They seized unmarried girls and children, grabbed things and money and in an instant they were [back] aboard their galleys, set sail and disappeared. The next day it was the same thing…"

As for Barbarossa? He died in Istanbul, in his bed at the age of 90, in 1546. The Turks constructed his tomb beside the Bosporus on the European side. For centuries, no Turkish fleet left the Golden Horn without the rolling thunder of their cannons as they passed the tomb, firing to salute their greatest seaman - the man who changed the Mediterranean.

Mediterranean coastal villages were forced to adopt a design of narrow alleyways (above right) and 'fortress churches' (above left) due to the constant threat of pirates. Note the ironwood door and lack of windows in the church on the left.

The Atlantic

Vikings in North America

He spoke with great conviction and authority. Blame it on the Labrador Current. Blame it on the reduced visibility, commonly known as fog. Blame it on an overly cautious nature. Not that it mattered. The MS *Veendam* was not going to Cartwright. The remote port in northern Labrador was scratched. Bypassed. Forgotten. The Captain had spoken.

It was hardly a surprise, or the first time. Although it was July, ice was riding the Labrador Current down from the Arctic. "Ice" was maritime jargon for the phrase most cruise ship passengers don't want to hear: iceberg. One tends to think of icebergs as massive chunks of ice, calved from great glaciers, which gradually reduce in size as they drift south. This is generally true. The berg which floats past the port side of the *Veendam* is almost as tall as the ship and much wider, but it wasn't the problem. The Captain was unconcerned with it as it was easy to track on radar. He was grousing about the growlers. Growlers were bergs which had mostly melted until only two or three feet were visible above water, but a huge chunk of ice was still present below. To collide with a growler meant a dent in the hull, or worse. They were hard to see. In foggy weather - impossible. The warm maritime air of the North Atlantic was flowing over the cold Labrador Current, causing the air to cool and condense: fog. So he was skipping Cartwright and turning east, charting a course clear of the ice field before he turned back to the north for Greenland.

Not that we, as passengers, were worried. We just wanted to make sure we had enough zoom on our cameras to capture some dramatic iceberg shots as we sailed by. Besides, the Captain had spoken; at sea there was no appeal. The weather thus far in our "Voyage of the Vikings" had been benign: calm seas, light winds, cool temperatures. A little ice now was not going to spoil the party.

Yet it was not always so on this route. When Bjarni Herjolfsson returned to Iceland from Norway around the year 985, he found his father's farm deserted. This was most distressing to young Bjarni. He inquired of the neighbors as to his father's fate. He heard the surprising news: his father had gone with Eric the Red to Greenland; he had joined the migration.

Eric the Red was an interesting and dangerous character. He had been exiled to Iceland from Norway for having a bad temper - a bad temper which had led to violence and death. While in Iceland, his temper had erupted again and again he was exiled. This time there was no place to send him. He left, sailing to the west, only to return the next year bearing stories of a great new land to the west. It was a land of opportunity, a land of potential. There were no people in the new land with whom to contend, plenty of fjords in which to fish, and plenty of arable land to farm or raise flocks. A beautiful land: it was called Greenland. Eric admitted later that he was stretching the point. But as any real estate promoter knows he needed a name for the new land which would attract settlers.

Attract settlers he did. Many who had settled late in the migration to Iceland were forced to accept farms which were poor possibilities: too rocky, too far from water, too exposed. A restart in Greenland had considerable appeal. Eric had put together quite a fleet of migrants and set out for western Greenland.

Bjarni wanted to be reunited with his father and so he polled his crew: would any go with him to Greenland? Adventurers all, they all agreed. He then asked if any had been to Greenland or knew the way. None replied. He inquired of the locals for the sailing directions to Greenland and set sail, never dreaming of his fate.

In the 10th century, ship navigation was very primitive. There was no compass, no sextant. Navigation was done by the stars at night and sun by day. The route to Greenland was virtually unknown as were the currents and the weather patterns. Only days out of Iceland, the wind shifted to the north and a dense fog set in. They sailed for days unable to get their bearings. Unbeknownst to Bjarni the north wind had pushed them far to the south; they missed Greenland altogether. They sailed on and on to the west. At last, Bjarni sighted land. It was low, hilly land covered with timber. It did not match the description of Greenland Bjarni had heard. He turned north and sailed two more days. Again he sighted land, but this was a low land with many trees. As Greenland was reported to be not forested, he refused to approach the coast. He sailed further north, approaching a land of great slabs of rock and ice. It did not look the least bit welcoming. Despite the crew's pleas for fresh water, Bjarni would not land. The land appeared harsh, barren; he wanted nothing to do with it.

Finally, after four more days of sailing, great mountains, topped by huge glaciers, appeared. Bjarni had found his Greenland. He stumbled across his father and found his new home. He was content.

What had Bjarni found? It's hard to say. The Sagas give us only a few clues as they were, after all, stories to be told by the fire in the evening, not a historical account. Undoubtedly, he had encountered the coast lines of Newfoundland and Labrador. The area to the north, his last encounter, particularly matches the Baffin Island area. No matter, Bjarni's story caused little comment and no excitement. For the Vikings trying to establish settlements in Greenland, the work was too hard and survival too tenuous to speculate over unknown lands to the west.

Here the Sagas take a time out. A number of years passed with little concern about the mystery to the west. But the mystery was not forgotten. Eric the Red's son, Leif the Lucky, was determined to sail to the west. Lief's great desire was to be successful like his father, to find a new land and plant a new colony. Such a successful effort would ensure that he was talked about by the fire in the evenings. Fame was almost as important to Vikings as wealth. He bought Bjarni's ship and enlisted Bjarni as a member of the crew.

Leif's ship of adventure was not one of the dramatic long ships whose very appearance terrorized Europe. Rather, it was a knorr, or trading vessel. Broad in the beam it appeared more like a tub than a sleek vessel deserving a dragon figurehead. It had a large area for cargo but its open decks afforded only a modest amount of comfort for the crew. Vikings were traders before they were raiders and the knorr was a well-built and reliable vessel.

Leif elected to sail Bjarni's route in reverse. When they left Greenland their course was directly west, reaching the area Bjarni had called Helluland. Even today the Baffin Island area has little to commend it. Leif found nothing of interest and turned south. Further south they encountered the area called Markland, an area of wooded hills and low sloping white, sandy beaches. Today tourist boards all over eastern Canada claim Markland for their own. There is some cachet about being part of Viking exploration, possibly because tourists like it. But none can know for sure where Leif landed.

For some unknown reason, Leif rejected Markland also and continued south. Leif's luck changed as they discovered an island. Venturing ashore they discovered large meadows and an even more pleasant surprise. The grass was covered with dew - dew the Vikings tasted and declared that they had never tasted anything as sweet. Intrigued by the island they sailed their ship into the sound between the island and the mainland. Here they encountered a great tide fall and went aground as the ocean raced out from beneath them. As the tide returned they rode it up a stream, then rowed into a lake of fresh water. Leif ordered sod houses built and sent out exploration teams. The area was heavy in timber, an important and valuable discovery. The streams swam with such salmon that they could be scooped out by hand. They decided to winter over here in this newfound paradise of plenty.

Where were they? Ah, that is the question. Even the name Leif gave the area is an enigma. Leif called the area Vinland. Here the Sagas let us down, confusing us for the rest of history. Some stories have the Vikings returning to Greenland with grapes and grapevines. Some, today, speculate that it was actually berries they found, but a larger question looms. In Old Norse the word "Vinland" can have two meanings. If the 'vin' in Vinland includes a diacritical mark (similar to an umlaut), then Vinland means wine or grapevine country. However. If the 'vin' is not accentuated by the diacritical mark the word means meadow or pasture. In the Sagas the Vikings remark how pleasant the land is and lush the meadows, that livestock could winter over without fodder. So, did they find a land of grapes or a land of meadows? The debate rages in academic circles but we will probably never know.

Leif and his fellow explorers successfully wintered over and returned in the spring to Greenland, their ship laden with America's first valuable cargo: timber. Greenland had no trees and the Greenland colonists were used to building everything, from homes to boats to furnishings, out of wood. Timber was extremely valuable to the colonists. Leif's expedition had been a success, not only in exploring new lands but returning with a valuable cargo.

Leif lost the urge to wander but his younger brother, Thorvald, was bitten by the exploration bug. Leif loaned him his ship and consented to the use of his houses in Vinland by Thorvald's expedition. Thorvald, though, was no Leif the Lucky. Thorvald had no trouble finding Leif's settlement, but he found something else, also: people. It is uncertain which indigenous people the Vikings found but one thing was for sure, they were deadly. The Vikings called these people the "Skraelings" or screamers.

Perhaps they were screamers because the Vikings were not the nicest of neighbors. Apparently, the Vikings encountered a fishing party of the Skraelings and simply killed them. Naturally, the locals were outraged. A very large party of Skraelings tried to ambush Thorvald and his men. In the fighting retreat, Thorvald took an arrow in the armpit. He lingered only long enough to give instructions for his burial near Leif's settlement. In the spring, Thorvald's men sailed home with another cargo of valuable timber.

Vikings were stoic but Thorvald's death grieved Leif's family. Leif's younger brother, Thorstein, volunteered to sail to Vinland. He promised to return Thorvald's body for proper burial in Greenland. Along with his wife, Gudrid, Thorstein recruited a crew and set sail. Alas, he was no Leif the Lucky either. A storm forced them ashore at a colony in southern Greenland. Here Thorstein caught the plague and died.

Adrift without a leader the expedition soon found an unlikely one: Karlsefni. Newly arrived from Iceland, Karlsefni had met the widowed Gudrid. It was not only love at first sight, but a melding of the minds. They married and recruited an even larger expedition to Vinland. Leaving Greenland with over 60 men and five women, plus numerous kinds of livestock, it was obvious that this expedition planned to stay in Vinland.

At first, things went well for the new colonists. They established a peaceful relationship and trade with the Skraelings. The land was rich, the weather was mild, and things were looking up. But the Skraelings were a Stone Age people to whom the metal tools and weapons of the Vikings represented wealth beyond imagination. They understood too well how much easier their life would be if they had metal. Pilferage of Viking tools and weapons began, which grew into open theft, which exploded into armed confrontation between the Vikings and the Skraelings. The Vikings always defended themselves well, warrior farmers that they were. But the constant low-level conflict with the Skraelings was tiresome and dangerous. Although the Vikings were better armed, the Skraelings vastly outnumbered them. No Viking could travel the forest alone, nor could they wander far from their village for fear of Skraeling attack.

After two winters it was clear to Karlsefni and Gudrid that there could not be peace with the Skraelings. The settlement could not prosper with the constant threat of fighting. They decided to return to Greenland. Interestingly, and unusual for these adventures, they took more persons back with them than they had brought. Gudrid had given birth to a son: Snorre. He was the first European child born in the New World.

So this ends the Viking Adventure in America? No. In the 1960s, Parks Canada took possession of a site in far northwest Newfoundland: L'Anse aux Meadow. This site, when excavated, revealed a small Viking way station or ship repair facility. It wasn't a full village, rather a stopping point. Although the Sagas grow silent after the adventures of Karlsefni and Gudrid, Viking trade with North America obviously did not end.

Vikings were traders before they were raiders. If nothing else, Vinland held the attraction of valuable timber. Greenland had no timber, the forests on Iceland were completely decimated and it was a very long way to Norway for wood. Vinland was closer. The colonies on Greenland lasted another 200 years before fading away to the cooling climate and pressure from the arriving Inuit. Trade with the peoples of the western lands, called Canada today, earned the Vikings walrus ivory and arctic furs, valuable in Europe. A trip to Vinland would easily yield a cargo of timber. While no more excavations in the New World have verified Vikings' presence, shipping logs in Iceland record the arrival, in 1347, of a ship filled with timber from Markland. Obviously hundreds of years before anyone heard of Christopher Columbus, the Vikings were regularly trading in and visiting North America.

Speaking of Columbus, one can only wonder what he heard in Iceland. While living and working in Lisbon with his brother, Christopher Columbus had made a trip to Iceland to participate in the stockfish (salt fish) trade. The Icelandic fishery was huge and profitable. Fish were in demand throughout Europe and the Columbus family was in the shipping business. Perhaps by the fire one evening in Reykjavik, someone began the story of Leif the Lucky or Karlsefni and Gudrid, or streams full of salmon and meadows of sweet dew? All in a new land. A land to the west.

Statue of Leif Ericsson in Reykjavik, Iceland

Mutiny on the Baltic

Association with history in the making, no matter how remote, seems a little strange, a little surreal. For instance, we all remember where we were when Neil Armstrong walked on the moon. Other major historical events have become stuck in our minds, enrolled in our memories over time. I remember where I was when the message came in.

My squadron was deployed to the Philippines at the time. The Cold War was at its height and we were busy keeping track of Soviet activities throughout Asia and across the Indian Ocean. I was the duty officer in the Operational Control Room when the message came in. Of course I couldn't read it; I couldn't even get a copy of it. I was simply notified that there was a message in the Communications Center for the Commanding Officer and the Commanding Officer only. An odd and unprecedented event. His curiosity running wild, the C.O. immediately went to the Comm Center to read the message. Since it was so restricted he couldn't really *tell* anyone the contents of the message. He would only mention an 'event' in the Soviet Navy in the Baltic. Of course, since it was so restricted the nature of the message was printed in *Time* magazine about six months later. Little did we know at the time what was transpiring on the far side of the world. And, to this day, neither the Soviets nor the Russians have admitted it.

The Navy of the Soviet Union was huge. It was not as technologically advanced as the American Navy, but it made up for that by being bigger - bigger in everything. Soviet ships generally carried more firepower than

American ships, more men than American ships, and there were more of them. Our story is of one ship, a Krivak class frigate named *Storozhevoy*, and a man named Stablin.

In 1975 Leonid Brezhnev was the General Secretary of the Soviet Union. His policies expanded Soviet influence worldwide, due to its growing military, but did it at the expense of economic prosperity at home. While the general population suffered with shortages, the party bosses were well cared for to the point of luxury. Much was the same in the Navy. Young conscripts had the worst of it, of course. Jammed like sardines into living quarters on board ship, they found their officers oppressive and the food depressing. Breakfast was oatmeal, lunch was potato soup, and dinner was oatmeal. Their work was menial. They were never trained for technical or responsible positions - these were reserved for the officers. The final insult was the constant and repetitive lectures on the merits of communism and the success of the Soviet Communist Party. Evidence of the failures of both was all around the conscripts. Morale was low.

The *Storozhevoy* was assigned to the Soviet Baltic Fleet. A Krivak class frigate meant she was slightly smaller than a destroyer, but still well armed with rapid firing guns, anti-aircraft missiles, torpedo launchers and rocket propelled depth bombs. She was small but lethal, and she had been busy. The *Storozhevoy* had spent much of her time at sea over the preceding year, much to the chagrin of the homesick sailors on board. The ship was a fertile breeding ground for discontent. That discontent, in turn, translated into performance in recent exercises which was so bad she had been singled out for criticism in the Soviet military newspaper *Red Star*.

The *Storozhevoy's* political officer was a mid-grade officer named Valery Stablin. A political officer in the modern Soviet Navy was no longer just a party hack, but also had to be a qualified naval officer. Although Stablin was third in command of the ship, he was behaving oddly as a political officer. When the young sailors complained of shipboard conditions or party failures, Stablin agreed with them. He sympathized with their plight and did the little he could to improve their lives. He also began quiet talks with several of the crew's leaders. He had a plan.

Much of what we know about what happened next we owe to an American naval officer named Gregory Young. Young was attending the Naval Postgraduate School in Monterey, California about eight years after the *Storozhevoy's* mutiny. He wrote a master's thesis on the subject, using only unclassified material. He solicited input from the Russian émigré community in the U.S. and had several strange telephone conversations with parties who wouldn't give their names but would give information. Fear of Soviet retribution reached all the way to the east coast of the U.S.

In November 1975, morale on the *Storozhevoy* had reached a new low. The ship, and most of the Baltic Fleet, was placed on alert as Soviet adventurism in Africa had raised tensions with the West. Leaves were cancelled and enlistments were extended. As a sop to the men, liberty was scheduled in Riga on November 7th, to commemorate the start of the Soviet Revolution. Stablin sensed an opportunity.

The celebration of the Glorious Revolution was always a big event. To Soviet sailors it meant liberty off the ship and liberty to consume huge amounts of alcohol. Alcoholism was a chronic problem in the Soviet Navy, as alcohol was used to drown the many problems and shortcomings of life. Stablin used this weakness to his advantage. Fully one half of the ship's 200 man crew would be off the ship on liberty that night, not expected to return until morning, if then.

The ship was tied up to the pier in the river in downtown Riga. It was a busy evening with a number of Soviet vessels in port and celebrating sailors everywhere. Stablin called a meeting of the officers remaining on board, explained his plan to take the ship, and asked who was with him. Several officers recoiled from the idea as lunacy. They were locked in their quarters. The captain had previously been lured below by Stablin and locked in a storage space. Stablin's plan took life.

At about 2 a.m. the ship cast off her lines and got under way. Moving even a small warship like the *Storozhevoy* requires the coordination of many people. The engine room must give the ship power, the bridge watch must properly navigate the ship in the channel, and the deck watch must properly cast off the vessel from the pier. Obviously Stablin had considerable help. But not all. As the ship moved down the river someone changed his mind about mutiny, jumped overboard, and swam for the shore.

Where were they going? What were they going to do? In 1975, it was assumed they were making a break for it, heading to Sweden to seek asylum and freedom. It would not be the first time. In 1961, another Soviet vessel had veered off course and taken refuge in Gotland Island, Swedish territory. The *Storozhevoy* was a very fast vessel, capable of speeds in excess of 30 knots. Once clear of the Gulf of Riga, Gotland Island was only five hours away. Was that the plan?

The Gulf of Riga is very shallow; ships must adhere to the channel to keep from running aground. Once beyond the mouth of the Gulf, the Baltic Sea opens into deep water affording more flexibility in maneuvering. The *Storozhevoy* steamed down the channel at high speed with her lights off, hoping to avoid detection. She had one more cloaking device going for her in her attempt to remain undiscovered: disbelief.

The swimmer had made shore and tried to alert the authorities. He received no help. At first he was simply viewed as another drunken sailor with a wild story. Finally reaching the naval base at Riga he told his story to the duty officer, who didn't believe him - until he checked. Sure enough, the *Storozhevoy* had left her berth. No orders had been issued to her. The local command tried to radio to her. There was no response. Puzzlement at the ship's activities had not yet turned to alarm. Besides, the local commanders were loath to admit that they had lost one of their warships. Just then the *Storozhevoy* cat leaped out of the proverbial bag.

The ship's radio sprang to life with an urgent message broadcast in Russian, but in the clear, not coded. It was a cry for help and a report that the ship had been hijacked: mutiny on board. One of the ship's officers had escaped from captivity and made it to the radio room. His message, broadcast in the clear, had been heard all over the Baltic region. There was no hiding it now. The Riga naval commanders went on full alert and telephoned Moscow.

Meanwhile, across the Baltic, the Swedish military had been enjoying the end of a quiet weekend. The late night hours were struggling to give way to early morning hours and the seasonal late sunrise. Then the entire eastern coast of the Baltic exploded. Soviet radars sprang to life all along the eastern coast of the Baltic. Radio channels, both air and sea, filled with chatter, both in the clear and coded. Swedish air defense radar started picking up air activity from Soviet bases. All of it was headed toward Sweden.

Moscow, as it could be imagined, was not about to be embarrassed by having one of its warships defect. Orders had come straight from the Kremlin to stop the ship. If necessary, sink it. No defection would be tolerated.

First aircraft into the air were units of Soviet naval aviation. It didn't take them long to locate a ship they thought to be the *Storozhevoy*. But it was dark - they couldn't be sure. When the Riga command ordered them to fire on the ship, the order was greeted by silence. The order was repeated and acknowledged but no action took place. Finally the naval aviation units were ordered home.

The naval aircraft were armed with large anti-ship missiles. These missiles certainly would have stopped the ship had they hit her. But they were fairly dumb weapons – once fired there was no control over the missile, it would home in on the target of its choice. What if that was the wrong ship? Air Force units were dispatched with bombs.

Meanwhile, naval units from up and down the coast were dispatched to pursue and stop the ship. One of those units was another Krivak class frigate. It was early morning in the November Baltic skies, barely light. The Air Force had found a target and was determined to stop it. They dropped a 500 pound bomb which struck the frigate and killed 33 sailors. It was the wrong ship. The

Navy finally convinced the Air Force that they were bombing the wrong ship and the search continued. Meanwhile, for some odd reason, Stablin had slowed his ship.

When only 21 miles from Gotland Island, the Air Force found the *Storozhevoy*. They dropped bombs close beside her and strafed the ship. Several sailors were killed by the strafing. Her rudder was jammed by the bombs and her engines damaged. The crew had had enough. They released the captain and the officers. Stablin was seized and an urgent radio message sent that the mutiny had ended, cease firing. Pursuing ships surrounded the *Storozhevoy*, marines boarded her, and everyone was arrested. The ship was towed back to port.

Stablin was whisked off to Moscow and trial. In a speedy trial, in which he was allowed no defense, Stablin was found guilty of treason and sentenced to death by firing squad. There was no appeal possible. Three days later he was executed and buried in an unmarked grave. It was three months before his family found out he was dead. When they asked for the body, they were refused by Soviet authorities. The excuse given was that the family had waited 'too long' to ask. One of Stablin's co-conspirators was sentenced to eight years at hard labor. Others faced military trial by the Navy.

What had happened? What were the mutineers up to? We can't be sure, but dueling theories have emerged. First, it was believed to be just another defection, although a spectacular one. Another theory emerged, courtesy of Gregory Young, 20 years after he had published his original master's thesis.

With the fall of the Soviet Union, Gregory Young was able to visit Moscow. He met with Stablin's wife and spoke extensively with her about the mutiny and Stablin. He met with others involved, and he formulated a new theory – the "good communist" theory.

It seems, since his youth, Stablin had been an advocate of communism and all it could do to help his country's ills. Indeed, while in the Navy he had taken the unusual step of transitioning to a political officer job instead of simply remaining a naval officer. He professed to want to help achieve communism's goals. During the Brezhnev years he became more and more disaffected with the failings of the old men who ran the Soviet Union. He clearly saw the failure of the Communist Party and bitterly resented it. He began to formulate an idea that others were likewise disaffected. In that he was correct. He thought if someone would issue a call to communist purity, a purge of the corruption and cronyism, the people would rise and rally to the cause. In this he was wrong.

He sought a symbolic act which would rally the people. What would be more symbolic than to seize the *Storozhevoy*, sail her to St. Petersburg, up the Neva River and anchor next to the *Aurora*. The *Aurora* had been the Russian cruiser, anchored in St. Petersburg in 1917, which fired her cannon to signal Russian patriots to storm the Winter Palace, seize the government, and proclaim communism. Stablin would anchor the *Storozhevoy* next to this icon, a historic ship museum, still in the river at St. Petersburg. He would then broadcast his appeal to all the Russian people to return to the purity of the Revolution and throw the rascals out of office. In his dream, the people would rally to his cause and do exactly that.

Is it even possible that he really thought this, or was it revisionist history put forth by a grieving family trying to rehabilitate a lost reputation? One can only guess. But the act itself would be impossible. Even if the ship had escaped the Gulf of Riga undetected, it would have to turn north in the Baltic and transit the Gulf of Finland. The Gulf of Finland is a fairly narrow and shallow body of water, easily patrolled and controlled. If he had made it to the St. Petersburg area he would have to transit the ship channel into the city. The channel begins next to a large Soviet fort and naval base: Kotlin Island. It would be impossible to pass Kotlin undetected. Once he entered the St. Petersburg area, he would have to transit the Neva River and pass under a variety of old bridges. As small as she was the *Storozhevoy* was still too large to fit under the bridges. Joining with the *Aurora* was simply impossible.

What had actually happened? Once clear of the Gulf of Riga, Stablin had not turned north for the Gulf of Finland. He had continued straight toward Gotland Island. But he had broadcast his manifesto, his call to revolution. He had it on tape and sent it over the ship's radio. Unfortunately for him, it went only to the military authorities. Was he a defector? A traitor? Or a revolutionary?

What of the Swedish and American governments? Both were officially silent as clams after the incident. The Americans were engaged in détente with the Soviets. They did not want to make statements which would embarrass the Soviets. Besides, they did not want the Soviets to know how much they knew or how they knew it.

As for the Swedes? Living next to a grumpy, hungry bear must be an uncomfortable life. One does not want to poke the bear. The Swedes had monitored the entire event using radar and radio. They had no comment. However, a persistent newspaper reporter, Alex Milits, had received calls from colleagues in Estonia, telling him to report on this story. Unfortunately, Milits had no facts. He badgered the Swedish government for some time over this story and continued to dig for facts. He finally published a story half a year after the event. But the big break, the expose, came when a Swedish journal accused the government of paying bribes to an American general. The government then had to defend itself by saying the payment they had made wasn't a bribe at all. It was payment for certain electronic eavesdropping equipment sold to them by the American military. It was the equipment they used to spy on the Soviets. They had not only inadvertently poked the bear, they had revealed some of their intelligence gathering methods. And they tacitly admitted the whole rumored affair of the *Storozhevoy* was true.

And the Soviets? They went to considerable lengths to make this a non-event. A target hulk was allowed to wash up on Swedish beaches to explain the bombing commotion as only an exercise. Another Krivak class frigate was repainted with the *Storozhevoy's* number and conspicuously sailed up and down the Baltic. Both damaged ships were repaired in a closed port with restricted access. The admiral in command of the Baltic Fleet was relieved of his duties. A year later the *Storozhevoy* was reassigned to the Pacific Fleet and sailed for Vladivostok, exiled to Siberia.

Was that the end of the story? Not exactly. A few years after he published his master's thesis, Gregory Young received a telephone call from an insurance salesman from New Jersey. He wanted to use part of Young's thesis as the basis for a novel he was writing. The novel was about a renegade Soviet naval commander who hijacked his own submarine. The writer's name was Tom Clancy. The book would become *The Hunt for Red October*. It, in turn, would become a movie of the same name starring Sean Connery. It would launch Tom Clancy on a career as a top military fiction writer. But, at the time, he wanted Young's story. He sensed that the truth, it seems, is stranger than fiction.

Soviet Union *Krivak* class frigate of the Cold War era

Courtesy of the U.S. Navy

Young Winston

It was a severe blow to Anglo-American relations. Our dinner companions were a British couple from the York area. We had been discussing jolly old England when Winston Churchill's name came up. In an offhand comment I happened to mention that "...he is half ours, you know. His mother was American." The effect on our companions was instantaneous and unforeseen. Our proper English lady's back stiffened, her smile straightened into a prune face, and her eyes locked on me like missile guidance: "That-has-nothing-whatever-to-do-with-it-of-course-he's-not-yours-he-is-ALL-ours". I attended closely to my soup.

The Winston that I was thinking of was not the short, pudgy fellow in the bowler hat, cigar, and 'V' symbol extended with his right hand. That's how many of us remember him, but it wasn't always that way. As a matter of fact, early in his life there was considerable doubt that he would ever attain any position of value.

Winston's father, Randolph, was the second son of the Duke of Marlborough. Second son was an unenviable position. His older brother would, upon the passing of the Duke, inherit not only the title but all the lands and wealth. Randolph would become a remittance man, on a stipend but never wealthy or with a real position in society. He would, however, be politely called 'Lord Randolph'. He had met Jenny Jerome at a party and was completely smitten with her; he had to have her. Jenny's mother had brought her daughters to Europe to meet royalty and marry them off to some wealthy aristocrat. Randolph would have to do.

The Duke was adamantly opposed to his youngest son's proposal to marry this girl for two reasons. First, well, she was an *American*, for heaven's sake. Secondly, her father was a *man of business*. These were not the type of people with whom the Churchill's normally associated. Randolph was persistent. The fact that Jenny had her own money and a dowry large enough to reroof Blenheim Palace, the Churchill's' historic home, helped turn the tide. They rushed to the altar and, seven months later, at Blenheim Palace, young Winston arrived.

Winston was born into a world of wealth, privilege, and power. He would live in an interesting time. He viewed the end of the Victorian Era in Britain, when the sun never set on the British Empire, and the breakup of that Empire over the next half century. Winston grew up in an indulged world in which 33,000 people held 80% of the wealth of the Empire. His father, Randolph, was elected to Parliament from a borough in which only 600 people were entitled to vote.

His parents, being aristocrats, were only modestly involved in the raising of young Winston. He was turned over to a nanny, Mrs. Everest, who doted on him and indulged him shamelessly. Naturally, he loved her dearly. His parents he knew only from afar. When the time came for Winston to go off to boarding school to learn his ABCs, he rebelled intensely. Boarding school was a great leveler of class and privilege. Each student had to not only learn but conform to the school's rules - something Winston hated. If he was interested in a subject, he could not learn enough. But if he was uninterested or bored with a subject, he could not be beaten, literally, enough to learn. His grades reflected the same. He professed not to care.

As he progressed into his teenage years, his grades failed to improve to the point that it was clear that he would never be admitted to a university. His father called a meeting. A normal son would have been crushed when told by his father how very disappointed he was in him, how he was a failure. But it was Randolph's admonition which failed. When told that there was little left for Winston to do but try for the Army, Winston lit up.

The Army! Randolph's censure failed to cool young Winston's ardor at the prospect of becoming an army officer. His ancestor, John Churchill, the first Duke of Marlborough, had been one of the most successful generals England has ever known. He was Winston's hero. As a boy, Winston was constantly playing with his toy soldier set, a set of 1,500 pieces. His younger brother, John, was forced to always command the French forces while Winston directed the Red Coats. Naturally the Red Coats won all the battles. The Army appealed to Winston, but there was a problem: his grades.

Admission to Sandhurst, the Army's training academy for potential officers, required demonstration of academic ability. Winston would have to pass a test. He was woefully unprepared academically, caused by his own neglect. His parents hired a 'crammer', a tutor who specialized in helping boys pass the Sandhurst test. It took three tries, but if nothing else Winston was persistent. Finally he was admitted.

The Army was good for Winston. He submitted willingly to its discipline, loved riding horses, and learned to play polo. After a year and a half of training, he graduated near the top of his class. He struck for the cavalry. His father refused.

Randolph knew that, in the real Army, the generals almost always came from the infantry. It was the way to the top. The cavalry was viewed as dashing and romantic, right enough, but not to be taken seriously. Besides, all those horses cost money. There was the work horse, the cavalry charger, but then each officer needed some ponies for polo, plus the attendant equipment. Money was something Randolph was short of and something Winston would always be short of. Winston held out and, in the end, won out. Commissioned into the cavalry his regiment was sent out to India for duty.

Regimental duty in Bangalore involved long languid days in the heat of southern India, and long rest breaks during the middle of the day to avoid the heat. Winston lived splendidly with other junior officers in what can only be described as a villa. A large household staff attended to all their needs leaving time on the young men's hands. Winston, in his conversations with other junior officers, began to sense what he had missed by not attending a university. He wrote to his mother who began shipping him crate after crate of books. Winston read voraciously. He began to quote Gibbon, and to write. And to develop ambition.

It is clear that Winston saw the Army as a stepping stone to greater things. He needed to do great things in the Army so that his name became known, so that he could point to his 'active service' record with pride. At the time, 'active service' meant combat. Unfortunately for his plan, there was no combat in southern India. There was, however, combat elsewhere.

A rebellion had broken out in the Afghan/Indian border region. The Army always expanded its officer corps in units engaged in combat, knowing that there would be casualties. Winston used his family influence to obtain one of the supernumerary openings in the command being sent to put down the rebellion. He performed well, was even "mentioned in dispatches". But, more importantly, he took a side job. Enroute to the front he solicited several English newspapers in India. He wanted to become their war correspondent, to report regularly on this campaign. Such an offer was a bonanza to the press. No serving officer had ever proposed such a thing. They readily accepted his offer. During the campaign he wrote well and his columns were well read, even in London. After the action he wrote a book, *The Story of the Malakand Field Force,* describing the event. It sold fairly well, remains in print today, and stands as a prescient description of Afghanistan and its troubles still, even in the 21st century.

Back with his regiment in Bangalore, Winston was, once again, bored. But not for long. Near the end of the 19th century it seems the Empire was almost always engaged in a struggle somewhere.   In Africa, the British government had changed its policy and decided to redeem the Sudan from its Muslim rebels. In this effort British Red Coats would support the Egyptian Army, which was led by British officers.

Winston, once again, used family connections to wrangle an assignment to the regular British cavalry unit assigned to this action. It was not easy. The commanding general, Kitchener, did not want him. Kitchener was well aware of Churchill's press connections. He wanted no junior officer second guessing his decisions in the London newspapers. Winston wrote to his mother, pleading with her to use her political connections on his behalf. He told her: "This is a pushing generation and we must push with the best of them."

Naturally, Winston won out. He obtained orders and sailed for Egypt, just in time to catch the last of the Army as it moved out up the Nile. His late arrival saved his life.

He participated in, and reported on, the major actions of the campaign. His press connections had not only survived but thrived. His reporting caused no little controversy as his views often differed from the Army's regular reports. The British Army would later change its policy – no active officer could henceforth work for a newspaper.

Winston rode in the last British cavalry charge in history, and was lucky to survive it. At the seminal battle of the campaign, at Omdurman, his regiment unwittingly charged a vastly superior force. Realizing the mismatch too late the regiment had no choice but to charge straight through the enemy. The regiment lost one-third of its men, dead and wounded, in the charge. Fate intervened for Winston. Because of his late arrival Winston had been given command of the last squadron in the regiment instead of his originally assigned squadron. The officer who took Winston's place was killed in the charge. Winston came through without a scratch.

His reports to the London newspapers were well read and, at the end of the campaign, he wrote another book. *The River War* sold well and convinced Winston that he needed a career change. He decided that, between his military service, his newspaper reporting and his books, he was well known. He resigned his commission from the Army and returned to London to stand for Parliament. He lost.

He now had no seat in Parliament. No army commission. And no job. Fortunately, what he did have was a war. In

South Africa, the Boers had risen against the policies of the British government. The Boers were well armed, well led, and highly motivated. They had pushed back the British Army everywhere, necessitating a relief force being sent out from England. Winston instantly obtained employment by the *Morning Sun* newspaper as their war correspondent and caught the convoy headed to South Africa. On board ship, he was something of a celebrity among the troops. He had seen active service, he had written books, he was a war correspondent. Not just a war correspondent, but undoubtedly the highest paid war correspondent ever and he was happy to share his largesse with anyone.

Upon arrival in South Africa, the Army went into camp to organize itself. Winston would brook no such inactivity. He and another reporter immediately caught the first train for the front. But they couldn't find the front. The situation was so fluid and the Boers moving so fast that nobody was quite sure where the front was. A worrisome situation; certainly not newsworthy.

After loafing around the leading British units for a few days, Winston met an officer with whom he had previously served. There was to be an armored train expedition tomorrow to reconnoiter toward the Boer lines, a probe to find the enemy. Winston's friend would be in command. Would Winston like to come along?

The next morning the train huffed into no-man's-land at first light. An armored train consisted of a locomotive, flat cars, and box cars. The locomotive was covered with steel sheets to protect it from enemy fire. Likewise, the box cars, where the troops rode, were lined with steel sheets for protection. Flat cars were pushed ahead by the locomotive, serving to detonate any mines set in the tracks by the Boers.

The train crept cautiously forward until mid-morning. Nothing was seen. They stopped at a small town to search for signs of the enemy. Nothing. The officer in charge decided they had come quite far enough and should return. They would report no enemy nearby. They were wrong.

The Boers had set a clever ambush. As the train rapidly returned, it rounded a hill only to find the Boers had placed large boulders on the tracks. Unable to stop, the lead cars struck the boulders and derailed. The train could now neither advance nor retreat. The Boers opened fire from both sides of the track with small arms and artillery. The situation was desperate. Winston offered to lead a work detail to clear the tracks if the Army would keep the Boers pinned down. Eagerly Winston gathered his work gang and rushed forward shouting: "Come on men, this will make a great story for my newspaper!"

Due to the lack of tools, manpower, and the heavy fire from the Boers, it took over an hour to clear the tracks. The wrecked cars were finally shoved aside, the wounded loaded onto the locomotive, and the engine began to move out of the deadly crossfire. Winston checked for stragglers, then ran after the locomotive. But the locomotive was moving too fast. He couldn't catch up. Still he continued running down the tracks, watching the train get further and further ahead. Fate intervened for Winston. He had left his pistol in the locomotive and was unarmed. As the Boers rode up they pointed rifles at Winston and simply said: "Hands up." Had he been armed they would have shot him. But he was now a prisoner.

Winston was confined with British army officers who were prisoners of war. They were all shipped north to Pretoria and confined in a school compound with a solid metal fence. With nothing but time on their hands, they did nothing but dream of escape. Some did more than dream. Winston and two officers carefully watched the compound's guards, hoping to find a weakness in the compound's security. They were determined to escape. They put together a plan and agreed to escape the next night.

After dark the next evening, the three potential escapees gathered near the fence. At the appropriate time, Winston scrambled over the fence. He hid in the shadows on the outside of the fence and waited for his friends. Nobody came over. Finally, after an eternity, a voice whispered through the fence: "We can't come, the guards are back. You need to come back." Winston was stunned.

He was not about to go back into captivity. He straightened his clothes, turned up his collar, and walked straight out through gloomy mist of the residential neighborhood surrounding his jail. He headed for the railroad yard. He knew his only hope was to make it to the sea. He must find a train heading east and ride it to the nearest neutral territory: Portuguese East Africa. Today, we call it Mozambique. It was almost 300 miles to safety, a very long way.

At the edge of town he hopped a slow moving freight and rode most of the night. Before dawn he slipped off the train to hide. He knew with the coming of morning would come role call at the prisoner camp. His absence would be noted and the alarm sounded. The trains would be searched. Patrols would be sent out. He was right.

The Boers knew exactly who Winston Churchill was. They knew he was a civilian, not an officer. Winston's cries that he was a non-combatant and couldn't be locked up had been laughed off by the Boers. They had seen him commanding the work crew at the armored train, and they knew his record. They were not about to let him go. Now, they laughed off his escape. They said: "A fat man with no hat has no chance on the veldt." But they posted a 25 pound reward for him, dead or alive. At the time, 25 pounds was enough money to induce almost anyone to turn him in. Almost.

After several days of walking by night and hiding by day, avoiding all civilization, existing on only a couple of chocolate bars, Winston came to the conclusion that the Boers were right, he could easily die out on the veldt. The rolling hills of the veldt prairie offered limited water, no food, and sparse shelter. He needed help. Desperation focused his mind. He determined that he would go to the next community, seek help, and perhaps turn himself in. He was fortunate in his choice.

After dark he approached a small mining town. Knocking on the door of the first house he encountered, a man with a gun came to the door. Fate, once again, intervened. As Winston struggled with a story the man simply said, "I know who you are," and dragged him into the house. The man was John Howard. Howard was the mine superintendent of the Transvall and Delgado Bay Collieries. He was British. At the start of the war, when the area was evacuated, he remained behind to keep the mine operating. His two miners were Scots. They hid Winston at the bottom of an abandoned mine shaft. The Boers were still actively searching for him but no one would search the bottom of a mine. After several days, they hatched a plan.

Howard brought in a neighbor, a Dutchman named Burgener. Burgener had a shipment of wool destined for the port of Maputo in Portuguese East Africa. They planned to load the wool onto rail cars at the siding next to the mine. Winston would be hidden in a small opening among the bundles of wool in the rail car. He would ride the wool car all the way to freedom.

A small space, a long trip, a wanted man? Winston had grave misgivings. It was a gamble, but Winston knew he couldn't sit at the bottom of a mine shaft until the end of the war. He hid in the train. Howard gave him food, water, and a pistol. The journey was not smooth: agonizing waits on sidings, switching of trains, long overnights with no movement. It took three days for the train to arrive at the border. The Boers searched the train enroute and again at the border, failing to discover the hiding place. Winston memorized the route to Maputo and knew all the stops. When he finally passed a station with a Portuguese name and saw Portuguese uniforms at the station, he knew he was out of Boer territory. He began singing and shouting, even fired off his pistol. Fortunately, the noise of the train covered his celebration.

Upon arrival at the rail yard in Maputo, Winston slipped quietly off the train and walked into town. To his surprise, Burgener was waiting for him. Burgener escorted him to the British Consulate where the Consul could not believe his luck. They gave him a bath, dinner, and an armed escort to the port. Maputo was filled with Boers and Boer sympathizers; the Consul was taking no chances on losing him. Winston's luck still held as the weekly steamer for Durban was leaving that evening.

Winston's escape and pending arrival at Durban were huge news stories. Up to this point, the war news had been all bad for the British. The daring adventure of a young man single-handedly baiting the Boers was the leading story. Upon arrival in Durban, Winston's steamer could not tie up to the pier as it was so crowded with well-wishers. Upon disembarkation he was greeted by the Mayor, the General, and the Admiral of the port. They asked if he wanted to say 'a few words' to the crowd. In a preview of things to come, Winston spoke for 30 minutes.

He was made now. Now he was famous, and through his own doing. He would pause again, signing on to the South African Light Horse as a cavalry officer. And a reporter. He was at many of the big battles and rode in the relief of Ladysmith. He also hardened his own credo – "In war – victory; in peace – magnanimity" - as he watched the harsh and unsuccessful British policy toward the Boers unfold.

He was, in reality, headed back to Britain. He stood for Parliament again in what he called the 'khaki election', which saw so many veterans voted into Parliament. Winston was one. From that point on, he was in Parliament almost the rest of his life. For the next half century, his hand hovered over many of the world's most important events. So it seems that the lady from York was partly correct in her dinner observation - he wasn't half ours. Fate had given him to the entire world.

Winston's toy soldier set. Churchill Museum, London

Fear of Bojador

Bojador meant fear. Fear is something, in its various shapes and forms, we all know. Fear is the dread of failure that haunts the professional athlete. Fear is the monster under the bed which frightens the small child. Some fear dogs or flying on airplanes. Some are not sure exactly what they fear, but are still fearful.

Courage, on the other hand, is said to be the antithesis of fear. We say one is courageous when one knows fear but goes ahead anyhow. Courage. Fear we know to be contagious. Is courage contagious, or is it so rare that is more rationed in mankind?

Cape Bojador meant fear. Perhaps it was the irrational kind, but some would certainly argue not. They would argue that a courageous man is not foolish. All the Portuguese sailors knew that to go to Cape Bojador was to die. Death was certainly something to fear.

Likewise, we pursue safety. We want it for our lives, and our family's lives. When the great Lisbon earthquake of 1755 struck, the shaking and undulating went on for almost 10 minutes. All knew fear then. Buildings all over town collapsed in heaps of rubble, crushing the unfortunates inside. Those trapped alive in the rubble faced the ghastly prospect of being consumed by the ensuing fires. Fear turned to panic. People rushed from their homes, their shops, looking for any open space that would ensure safety from the falling structures and the fires sweeping inexorability across the city.

Thousands rushed to Palace Square, the huge open plaza next to the King's home, Royal Ribeira Palace. The Square, bordering the north side of the broad Tagus River, was the commercial center of the city. Large government office buildings, in the new Manueline style, surrounded the Square, impressive in their size and majestic strength. Here in the arms of wealth and power, the people felt safe. They were wrong. Many went on board ships anchored just off the Square, seeking safety afloat. They were wrong also.

About a half hour after the shaking stopped, the people noticed the Tagus River starting to flow in reverse. Water was leaving the harbor; the harbor bottom became exposed. Ships grounded on their sides with no water left to support them. People walked out into the harbor to walk on the harbor bottom. Then they saw it - a huge wave rushing up the river bed from the sea. Perhaps twenty feet high it swept into the Square washing all before it. Huge cargo ships were thrown up into the Square. Government buildings were undermined and collapsed. The wave swept everything before it. People and debris were washed further and further inland. Then it retreated. It retreated carrying thousands of victims, tons of debris, and the heart of Portugal with it. It would return twice more to finish the job.

What the earthquake did not wreck and the tsunami wash to the sea, the fires consumed. Burning for five days, almost 85% of Lisbon was destroyed by fire. Untold thousands lost their lives. Untold because there were no records left to record their misery. The Palace was destroyed. The Royal Library with its 70,000 volumes, destroyed. The Royal Archives, inside the Palace, destroyed. Here we are robbed; robbed of the opportunity to detail this great tragedy. Also robbed of the opportunity to know of one of mankind's greatest adventures, greatest acts of courage: the Age of Exploration. Also to know of the Portuguese heroes: Prince Henry the Navigator, DeGama, Gil Eanes, Dias, and the others.

Portuguese lore says that Prince Henry established a school for navigators in the south of Portugal at Sagres, a remote, windswept spot far out on a peninsula. He is, today, honored for his leadership in navigation and exploration. Some say Prince Henry never went to Sagres, or if he did he certainly never established a school. Perhaps we will never know. Today academics fight like cats over whether Henry's school of navigators ever existed. There is no record of it, only stories. It is certain that Henry brought one of Europe's most imminent map makers to Portugal to teach the construction and use of nautical charts and maps. It is also certain that Henry studied the stars and encouraged others to do so.

Henry was the third son of the Portuguese King John and his English wife Phillipa. Completely loyal to his elder brothers, Henry never sought the throne, but sought his life elsewhere. Henry hungered for two things: first, to expand Christendom. He was a devout Catholic known to actually, on occasion, wear a hair shirt. He wanted to bring the true religion to infidels and heathens around the world. His piety was so renowned that the Pope appointed him as Master of the Order of Christ, the remnant of the Knights Templar. Secondly, he wanted to expand Portugal. A small country of little relative wealth, Portugal's only hope was through the sea. Practically astride the Strait of Gibraltar, it was perfectly located to be a major player in trade between the Mediterranean and northern Europe. Unfortunately the lucrative trade from Africa and the East was literally owned by the Muslims of North Africa and the Levant. Their trading partner was the Venetian Republic, ruthless merchants who brooked no competition. The trade in spices and goods from the Orient had made both sides wealthy beyond belief. Henry saw that trade and yearned.

During the Portuguese invasion and conquest of Cueta in northern Morocco in 1415, Henry had seen the wealth for himself. Thousands of sacks of spices of every variety, ripped open and scattered by Portuguese troops, had been everywhere in Cueta. The troops had been seeking riches. The riches were there, scattered at their feet, but the troops were too plebian to understand. Henry looked at the spices and the richness of this city of spices and understood. For Portugal to acquire wealth, Portugal must acquire trade.

What did he do now? Historical certainly is lost not only to the earthquake and tsunami of 1755 and the destruction of records, but also to the wall of secrecy surrounding Henry's ideas and accomplishments. Secrecy of the Portuguese technical advances was complete as, early in the 15th century, the Portuguese had every right to fear their Spanish neighbors and the great European trading states such as Venice.

As Henry pondered the problem, he understood that access to the East via the eastern Mediterranean was blocked by Venetian and Muslim interests. Nothing was known of what lay the other direction, toward the setting sun, except vastness. Perhaps if the Portuguese ventured south they could find trade with those peoples from whom the Muslims were obtaining their spices and gold. More importantly, perhaps they could find Prester John.

Prester John was said to be the ruler of a Christian kingdom somewhere in Africa, or perhaps it was Asia. No one knew for sure. But just as surely as they believed in sunrise, Christians of the era believed in the existence of Prester John. He was a descendant of one of Christ's disciples who had journeyed eastward and established a Christian kingdom, only to be cut off from Europe by the rise of the Muslims.

No such person or kingdom ever existed, but the rumor was its own truth, not to be denied. Linking with Prester John was thought to not only strengthen Christendom, but also give Europeans a friend in the East, which could only enhance trade.

Henry decided the path the Portuguese should pursue was to the south. As a duke, Henry had not only the authority to send ships to the south, he had the money to pay for the ventures. He was the Governor of the Algarve, the south of Portugal. He collected the customs duties from the busy port of Lagos. He held a monopoly on the manufacture and sale of soap in Portugal, and he had the revenues from the Order of Christ. Money he had, or could get.

Here, Henry's high hopes collided with harsh reality. Virtually nothing was known of sea routes to the south. The Portuguese had sailed the Mediterranean completely and ventured to northern Europe, but south? No. These men of the sea paid no heed to stories that the world was flat or that monsters at sea swallowed ships. They knew those fears to be false. They did know they had questions, serious unanswered questions, about the way south. The Portuguese had crept, cautiously and slowly, south along the west coast of Africa. Each year, the voyages went a little further south.

What would happen as they approached the equator? Some worried the ships would melt, literally, or at least the tar serving as chalking would melt letting in the sea. Others thought the heat of the sun could cause the sea to boil. More practical worries were mundane and deadly: where would they find fresh water on such a voyage? No one knew.

What they did know was that the coast to the south, the west coast of Africa, was terrifically hot, and filled with shallows and shoals. The African continental shelf extended well out to sea making the sea shallow and subject to shifting sand bars. And ship wreck? No hope. If one made it ashore all that could be seen was desert. Any hope of water would come only from the Muslims, who would be happy to give shipwrecked sailors water as they marched them off to the slave market for sale. The sailors preferred to contemplate sea monsters to such a fate.

To avoid the shallows of the coastline they could sail far out to sea. But no one understood how to sail for days out of sight of land. Better navigation instruments and skills would be needed.

His captains presented Henry with another problem: their ships were too small. To sail far to the south was a journey of many weeks, perhaps months. The ships they were sailing, the barcas, had served well in the Mediterranean but were simply unsuited for the Atlantic. They were beamy, single-masted vessels, unhandy in adverse winds and weren't even fully decked. The crew was continually exposed to the elements and there was no room to store enough water. To die of thirst on an ocean of water was the ultimate irony no one wished to contemplate. Even if they could store water, where would they store cargo in sufficient quantity to pay for the voyage? A new type of ship would be needed.

Still, there was Cape Bojador. Or the fear of Cape Bojador. Not much of a cape, in modern view, it's not the most prominent in western Africa or even the westernmost, but it was the most feared. Bojador stuck out like a thumb, a killing thumb, into the Atlantic. The seas washing it were shallow. So shallow, and impregnated with submerged reefs, that the swift current flowing over the reefs made the water seem to fly out of the sea, even on calm days. The shallow sea was alive with sardines also. When the large fish were feeding, the sardines flew to the surface to escape. Their huge numbers and frantic efforts to escape the large predators made the sea seem to boil. And the land of Bojador? Desert. Desert everywhere, a world of brown. No green in sight anywhere. A hot world of brown, the color of Morocco. Small wonder that men, 700 nautical miles from home, suspicious, superstitious, hot, and cautious, imagined that the surface of the sea was boiling. Look, there is the steam!

They were pragmatic, those seamen. They needed a reason - an explanation as to why those who had gone south of Cape Bojador had never come back. A boiling sea would do. In reality, it was the contrary winds, swift and adverse currents, shallow reefs, storms and shipwrecks which had done those early explorers in. But nobody knew. Pragmatic seamen knew that they had gone 700 miles already and must go 700 miles to return. Would they have enough food? Enough water? Better to be safe and turn around now.

Henry had heard all of these excuses about why the Portuguese could sail no further south, and he tired of them. He summoned Gil Eanes. Eanes was a trusted man, a man who had been a captain for Henry for 10 years. Henry told Eanes he would give him a ship, but his job was to go as far south of Cape Bojador as he could sail. Not go to Bojador, but go as far south of it as possible. Eanes humbly, and with trepidation, accepted his charge and sailed. Only to return and report that it was impossible to sail south of Cape Bojador. Henry was undeterred.

The next year, 1434, Henry summoned Eanes again. It was supposed that Henry offered Eanes an inducement, a very large inducement, if he would round Cape Bojador and sail south. Whatever it was, it was enough to convince Eanes to try again. If every man has his price, then so does courage. This time Eanes would try something differently. Instead of hugging the coast he stood well out to sea. Here he found the winds more variable and favorable, the current steady. He rounded Bojador and sailed as far south as he dared. He had slain the sea monster of fear that was Cape Bojador. He then turned around to carry the news to Henry, and to carry other news, too. If they were going to explore further south, they would need bigger and better boats. They needed to borrow from the Muslims.

An improvement over the barca would be a technological advance. The square sail and tubby build of the barca made it unhandy close inshore. It was impossible to sail with the wind other than astern. The Muslims, on the other hand, used a triangle shaped sail hoisted out on a very long yard or arm. These ships, the dhows, with their triangular sail, could sail with the wind astern or on the beam. The dhows were known throughout the eastern Mediterranean and across the Indian Ocean. They had conducted the spice trade between India and Arabia for hundreds of years. Dhow was not an Arabic term, rather the Arabs referred to this vessel as a qarib or "mule". The steady wind of the Indian Ocean monsoon made a passage to India not only easy but pleasant during the season of the southwesterly. Likewise, the return voyage with southeasterly breezes required little tacking as the winds were constant. The Portuguese knew that, for the Atlantic, a ship would have to tack, sometimes often, to handle the variable breezes of the different latitudes.

The Portuguese captains determined to adopt the triangular sail, but place it on a shorter yard making it easier to come about, or change course. They also elected to place a second mast on this new vessel, giving them redundant propulsion in case one sail or mast was lost. It also afforded them the opportunity to hoist two sails at once for greater speed. They decided to place a fixed rudder on the stern of the ship. The rudder would replace the large steering oar of the barca. The rudder would make the ship more manageable as it was larger than the oar and would not pop out of the water in heavy seas like the oar. The ship was refined, narrowed in her beam. Instead of a tubby affair, the new type ship would be narrow and sleek. Sleek, fast, and maneuverable, the ship was dubbed the caravel. It would be the standard of sailing fleets for hundreds of years.

The caravel would be fully decked, protecting people and cargo below. A second deck would be built on the stern providing quarters for the officers. As years passed more decks would be added both forward and aft serving a variety of purposes. For now the caravel was the answer to an exploring captain's prayer.

By 1440, the caravels had put to sea. They literally sailed past Bojador on the following currents and winds. They discovered that, further south, Africa was green, and the land of the black men, not the Arabs. They would then stand far out to sea to pick up the variable winds which carried them home or at least to the Madeiras.

So, what of Henry's school? Did it teach these men to sail or to navigate? Probably not. It probably wasn't a school at all, but more of a caucus of seamen or information exchange. Henry pressed his captains to do more, sail further. In return, the captains exchanged ideas about navigation devices such as the quadrant. The quadrant would turn into the sextant in the following centuries, but for now captains used it only to mark the latitude of familiar places such as Funchal or Lagos. What of Henry's chart maker? Charts were the heart of the Portuguese exploration. Each year as the captains returned from their voyages south, more and more of the unknown coast of Africa was detailed on the Portuguese chart of West Africa. This chart was a terrific secret and closely held by the Portuguese. Why? Did they discover something? The rest of the world could only wonder, particularly when Henry approached the Pope seeking a Papal bull giving the Portuguese the exclusive right to trade in and colonize West Africa.

It would be misleading to think of the Portuguese as merely explorationists when they were, at heart, merchants. The long voyages were to trade for gold, spices, and, in the end, slaves. Slave trading with the West African tribes was the black heart of Henry's enterprise. After the discovery of Brazil and its vast reaches requiring labor, the Portuguese slave trade exported over six million people from West Africa as slaves over the next three centuries.

By the time of Henry's death in 1460, the Portuguese had rounded the great bulge of Africa and were sailing east, still exploring. They had set up trading posts all along the African coast; the profits were modest but steady. They paved the way for the Portuguese moon shot of the 15th century – the route to India. DeGama would lean upon the knowledge gleaned by the early Portuguese captains of winds and currents, watering stops, and hostile tribes. Once past the Cape of Good Hope, he would be on his own but the Portuguese had grown bold in long distance navigating and the sailing of their swift, maneuverable caravels. The Route to India enriched Portugal beyond its wildest dream. It caused Brazil to be discovered. It also humbled the Venetians and the Arabs and emboldened the British and the Dutch. In short, it changed the world.

Was Henry's "school" for navigators the cause of all this? We may never know. Secrecy and earthquakes have hidden much of the record of these voyages from us. However, one never knows - deep in an archive somewhere in Europe may be a book, a box, or a logbook, the record of Portugal's courageous past. We should not fear to search for it, to explore for the hidden past.

Prince Henry the Navigator

Maritime Museum, Lisbon

The caravel – this newly designed vessel revolutionized European sailing and enable the "Age of Exploration". Maritime Museum, Lisbon.

Volcano in the Back Yard

It seemed appropriate to name the islands after those who had fled there for their lives. The Vikings referred to Celts and Saxons as "westmen" because, in the Viking view, they lived to the west: in England, Scotland, and Ireland. So, in the ninth century, the small islands off the south coast of Iceland were called the Westmann Islands after their most infamous occupants. The Viking immigration to Iceland had just begun with the more prosperous Vikings leading the way. With them they brought their family, friends, and slaves.

Vikings had always believed in slavery, either as a matter of commerce, the sale of slaves being very lucrative, or as a matter of practicality. Farming was labor intensive and slaves enabled the Viking farmer to be much more productive. The slaves, however, did not care for it. So much so that, from time to time, slaves would run away, or turn on their master - which is exactly what happened to Hjorleifr Hrodmarsson. He had a reputation for mistreating his slaves. His Irish slaves resented it. Now, virtually alone in a new land, the slaves rose up and killed him. They fled for their lives to the small volcanic islands about seven miles south of the coast of Iceland. It was not to be a refuge. Viking vengeance followed them. None the less, the islands were named for those westmen fugitives.

After that bit of excitement, things unwound rather quietly in the Westmanns for the next thousand years. It would not always be so. Nature had placed Iceland, and the Westmann Islands, astride what geologists called a spreading center. Here, two of earth's giant surface plates meet – the North American Plate butts against the Eurasian Plate. The plates are, slowly, going different directions, spreading away from each other. However, nature abhors a vacuum, and as the plates pull apart nature supplies magma from the asthenosphere, deep under the plates, to fill in the void. This process is called land building as new surface of the earth is created by the upwelling magma. Sometimes the magma gets out of control.

By the 20th century, the people of Iceland had come to rely on the Westmann Islands, particularly the island of Heimay and its principle town of Vestmannaeyjar. The shallow waters to the south of Iceland were alive with fish. The influence of the nearby Gulf Stream waters in warming the cold north Atlantic waters made this area the most important fishery in Iceland. Vestmannaeyjar had grown over the centuries simply because it was the best harbor facility available to the fishing fleet. Best is a relative term when dealing with the north Atlantic. Here, the harbor was protected on three sides by the island, but still open to the ocean to the east. A breakwater was constructed to help shelter the fishing fleet in the harbor.

The fishing fleet had grown in the 20th century due to the advent of the motorized fishing boat. Fishing that had taken a week by rowing boat or sail could now be accomplished in a few days. Fishermen could travel further, more safely, and carry more catch. Refrigeration allowed for the processing of more fish. All of this progress combined to make Vestmannaeyjar not only the best harbor in the south of Iceland, but also Iceland's most important fishing port.

The town had grown with the fishing fleet until it numbered over 5,000 people. The dock area had grown as well with the establishment of warehouses and fish factories to support the fleet. No one paid much attention to the fact that the island was of volcanic origin. The old cinder cones south of the town were viewed as little more than relics of the past. Besides, scientists and government officials had all concluded that the old Helgafell volcano, asleep for 5,000 years, was not only dormant but probably extinct. They had forgotten that geological phenomenon slumber at rates not understood by man.

It is true that, throughout its history, Iceland has experienced dozens of major volcanic events. All of these have been located along its volcanic zones and active volcanoes were the culprits in virtually all of them. Spectacular some of them were: the 2010 eruption of Eyjafjallajokull cast volcanic ash 35,000 feet into the air and disrupted air travel between North America and Europe for a week. The eruption below the Vatnajkull Glacier caused massive melting of the glacier and widespread flooding. The 18th century eruption of Skaftareldar resulted in the starvation of a quarter of the population of Iceland due to its destruction of crops and livestock.

Interestingly, Helgafell slept through all of these events, and stirred to life slowly - a languid awakening. It started on a quiet Monday evening. A swarm of minor seismic events, earthquakes, started, one following rapidly on the heels of the other. None were earth shattering or even earth shaking. Most were in the range of around 2.6 on the Richter scale, hardly noticeable to humans, but certainly measureable by geologists. Unfortunately, at the time, there was no effective seismic warning system in place. Magma had begun pushing toward the surface and doing so gently, almost as if it was trying not to wake the sleeping population.

Fortunately, the fishing fleet was in the harbor that evening, refugees from a typical North Atlantic gale. With winds blowing to 12 on the Beauford scale, the ocean was no place for a fisherman. The winds had blown hard out of the southeast, even roiling the waters in the harbor. Fortunately enough, the gale had passed by and the winds shifted to the southwest and moderated. Both events would save the town. And its people.

By late in the evening of January 22, 1973, the town was asleep. The first official notice that something amiss was a telephone call to the police at 1:55 a.m. The astonished caller seemed to be reporting a volcano erupting on the southeast side of town, just beyond the church farm. An officer was dispatched to the outskirts of town. Sure enough, the astonished officer confirmed what the astonished caller had reported: a volcano was erupting, and right in town, too. A long fissure had opened, spouting multiple fountains of fire and stretching as far as he could see.

The fissure, over a mile long, had opened only a quarter a mile from the center of town. The fissure ran in a northeasterly direction and seemed to cut that part of the island from shore to shore. Molten magma, bright yellow and red, shot out all along the fissure in a curtain of fire a mile long and up to 375 feet high. The effect was spectacular, if frightening.

The town was shaken from its slumber by the blaring of the town's fire alarm. Police and fire vehicles drove through the town streets, sirens moaning and shrieking.

Driven from their beds by the noise Vestmannaeyjar's population was soon awake, astonished, and moving.

The lava flow from the fissure was moving in a northeasterly direction, not yet threatening the downtown area. But the fissure was erupting a tremendous amount of tephra, or volcanic ash. Fortunately, this cloud of hot rock particles was being blown mostly out to sea by the same gale which had just passed the island.

As the lava flow was into the sea outside of the harbor, and the extent of the fissure to the northeast could not be ascertained, the town's leaders feared that the harbor may eventually become blocked. There would then be no escape by sea. The decision was made immediately to evacuate the town's population of 5,000. Fortunately, almost the entire fishing fleet was in port. People, carrying only a minimum of their belongings, began to go on board the fishing boats. The first boat left for Iceland at 2:30 a.m. A steady stream of fishing boats left the harbor in an orderly procession for the short trip to Iceland. The Icelandic government had been notified; airlines at Reykjavik and the NATO military at Keflavik were alerted. The small airport at Vestmannaeyjar was soon busy with flights removing the sick and aged. By late morning almost the entire population of the island had been evacuated. Only about 500 essential service personnel remained behind.

The volcano seemed to do whatever it wanted. From a spectacular fire curtain, it developed into a smoky cloud, then concentrated on building a new cinder cone just behind the destroyed church. The cone rose to a height of over 300 feet. Lava bombs, expelled high into the air above the volcano, rained down on the town and started fires on many structures. Volcanic ash fell in huge quantities in town, blocking the streets, and covering buildings. Over the next several days, the force of the volcano waxed and waned. Geologists kept close watch on the volcano and noted the lava begin flowing into the harbor. Harbor water temperatures reached over 110 degrees Fahrenheit. Smoke and volcanic ash were ejected as high as 22,000 feet above the volcano. And the volcano had a new name: Eldfell or 'Fire Mountain'.

Eldfell would be very hard on its neighbor Vestmannaeyjar. By the end of the eruption over 300 buildings in the town were destroyed by the lava flows, and 60-70 homes completely buried under the volcanic ash. Yet all was not lost. Geologists monitoring the eruption began to form a plan. They noted that the lava flows were relatively viscous and slow moving, traveling only about three to nine yards per day. If they could control the direction of the lava flow, they might be able to save part of the town and the waterfront area. They experimented by using fire hoses to attack the sides of the lava flow. It was apparent the lava could be cooled sufficiently to cause it to harden at ground level. This caused the lava behind the leading edge to mound up upon it and form a hardened wall. More water was needed.

The Icelandic government endorsed the idea. More water lines were set up and, just two weeks after the eruption began, the cooling project got underway in earnest. Later, a pump ship which could move large volumes of water was brought in. As the program advanced, large capacity pumps were leased from the U.S. and attached to a variety of portable water lines on and near the lava flow. Large volumes of water were sprayed on lava areas well behind the flow front. As these areas cooled, they solidified. The lava was coming from the volcano at temperatures around 1,900 to 2,000 degrees Fahrenheit. But, as it turns out, basalts start to solidify and harden once their internal temperatures drop below 1,500 degrees. As the lava cooled and solidified, bulldozers were brought in to cut roads across the lava. New water lines were laid on the roads and the water assault continued further across the lava flow. As fresh flows from the volcano met the solid lava, it tended to heap up behind the solid wall, not flow under or around it. The lava arrested itself.

The effort was vital to the salvation of Vestmannaeyjar. One lava flow threatened to fill the harbor and had to be diverted out to sea. Another had to be blocked from entering the downtown area and the residential area. The effort employed 75 men around the clock for months.

Finally, around the first week in July, Eldfell drifted off to sleep again. The lava flows abated and then stopped altogether. It appeared that in the epic struggle of man versus the volcano that man had actually won. The harbor had not only been saved but the diverted lava flows had pushed offshore and caused a natural breakwater. It provided more protection for the harbor from the open sea than anyone had dreamed. The best harbor in the south of Iceland was now even better. Plus, the small island of Heimay had gained an additional square mile of land surface, all courtesy of Eldfell. But what a mess.

Volcanic ash fall had simply buried whole houses and buildings. Others had burned out. Streets were impassable due to the ash and lava. On many buildings the roof had collapsed due to the weight of the ash. An entire section of town had been destroyed by the lava. Fully one-third of the homes and buildings of the town had been lost to the volcano. But Icelanders would prove, once again, that they do not shrink from adversity. People began filtering back into town. By summer, many were back and busy with cleanup and reconstruction efforts. It was decided that schools would open in the fall. Some residents never returned to Vestmannaeyjar but in their places came other hardy souls eager to participate in the rebuilding. A decade after the eruption the population of the town was almost the same as the pre-eruption population.

Previously, Heimay had suffered from a shortage of building material. Now it was present in tons. Some of the ash was used as a base to extend the runway at the airport. Many of the new homes constructed to replace those lost to the volcano were done so on a base of volcanic ash. Then there was the heat issue.

Iceland heats fully 85% of its structures today with geothermal heat. Previously, Vestmannaeyjar had not been able to benefit from this technology due to its cost and availability. Now they had over a mile of slowly cooling lava fields with which to heat their water. Pipe was run down into the lava. Water was pumped through the pipe and heated by the lava. As steam returned, it passed through heat exchangers to heat the water and homes of the population. Eldfell was slumbering but in a beneficial way.

Iceland is filled with Norse traditions. The Sagas are replete with stories of heroic struggles against fearsome odds, of monsters and trolls, and of nature run amok. It would appear that, on occasion, there may be a shred of truth in the Sagas. Iceland is a land of fearsome beauty carved by nature: glaciers gouge giant fjords; volcanoes build and destroy huge mountains; lakes of hot water defy winter's grip. Iceland's people? Over the years - fearless. It is well that this is so. Only the fearless could fight back against a fire breathing monster in their backyard, and win. At least for now.

A geyser erupts in one of Iceland's geothermal zones.

About the author

Captain Paul Eschenfelder has spent years entertaining and informing thousands of cruise ship passengers around the world. As a lecturer for a half dozen cruise lines he has spoken on a variety of subjects regarding regional history, culture and adventure. His forty years in the air around the world, plus years at sea as a lecturer, have found him bargaining with the Masai in Kenya, tripping over antiquities in Greece and Ireland, and benefiting from the spirit of ohana in Polynesia. A former lecturer at the University of Texas and adjunct professor at Embry Riddle Aeronautical University, he has served as an advisor to governments from Canada to Columbia and appeared on a variety of television and radio news programs. His written works have been published in a number of professional journals. He is retired as a captain for Delta Air Lines and a pilot for the U.S. Navy.

See more at: www.captaincruising.net

503.840.8232